Writer to Writer

Fluency and Craft in the Multilingual Classroom

Mary Lee Prescott-Griffin

HEINEMANN
Portsmouth, NH

Heinemann
A division of Reed Elsevier Inc.
361 Hanover Street
Portsmouth, NH 03801–3912
www.heinemann.com

Offices and agents throughout the world

Library of Congress Cataloging-in-Publication Data
Prescott-Griffin, Mary Lee.
 Writer to writer : fluency and craft in the multilingual classroom /
Mary Lee Prescott-Griffin.
     p. cm.
  Includes bibliographical references.
  ISBN-13: 978-0-325-00878-3
  ISBN-10: 0-325-00878-7
 1. English language—Composition and exercises—Study and teaching
(Elementary)—United States. 2. Group work in education—United
States. 3. Multicultural education—United States. I. Title.
  LB1576.P726 2007
  372.62'3—dc22   2007019286

Editor: Kate Montgomery
Production service: Denise A. Botelho
Production coordinator: Sonja S. Chapman
Cover design: Night & Day Design
Compositor: Aptara, Inc.
Manufacturing: Steve Bernier

Printed in the United States of America on acid-free paper
11 10 09 08 07 VP 1 2 3 4 5

To my sisters, Betty, Pamela, and Louise Prescott.
For all the hours spent as my "first pupils" and so much more!

Contents

Acknowledgments

In truth, I am simply an observer and note taker. Teachers and students are the ones who "write" my books, their collective wisdom and brilliant mentoring of one another providing both the inspiration and content of my work. So it is with this book about writing partnerships. When I visit classrooms and listen to the talk, teacher-to-student and student-to-student, I am awed by the innovative, original approaches to teaching I witness. With every visit, I come away with skills, strategies, and ideas to use in my own writing as well as content and substance for books such as this one. So, first, I want to applaud, thank, and acknowledge all the teachers and students with whom I work in my job as education professor at Wheaton College in Norton, Massachusetts, specifically those individuals who have welcomed me again and again into their classrooms to observe and converse about reading, writing, and collaboration.

I am also indebted to the writers of all ages at the L. G. Nourse and Solmonese Elementary Schools in Norton, Massachusetts; Spencer Borden School in Fall River, Massachusetts; Paul Cuffee Charter School in Providence, Rhode Island; Mills Pond Elementary School in St. James, New York, Woodingdean Primary School in Woodingdean, England and the Treasure Box Preschool in Singapore. It is their actions, words, and original strategies that teach me most. In the heat of their literate interactions, they continue to expand and define my understandings about learning in social context.

Sincere appreciation and profound respect also go to extraordinary teachers Sharon Roberts, Kristine Kefor, Cheryl Feeney, Christine Mikalyzk, Darline

Berrios, Emma Smith, Juvine Lee Wei Ping, Thiruchelvi Dio Rengasamy, Kelly Barr, Heather Stonehill, Jenny Baumeister, Seth Paster, Missy Taylor, Jeanne Hall, Cynthia Pasieka, and Diana Lanze, who opened their classroom doors, generously sharing their expertise as well as their successes and challenges in implementing writing partnerships. Thank you, too, to their administrators— facilitative leaders Lynda Ashley, Vivian Ang Sok mei, Mary Brown, Josie Woollam, David Bourns, Suzie Shaw, and Arlene Wild— who never say "no" when I propose "yet another research visit" to their schools. I am grateful for their time in arranging classroom visits and scheduling teacher and student interviews.

As always, I am so appreciative of the work every one with Heinemann— Sonja Chapman, Eric Chalek, Denise Botelho, and Dusty Leigh as my books move from manuscript to print and beyond. Their care and attention make the publishing process a pleasure, especially the work of my editor, Kate Montgomery, and her assistant, Kerry Herlihy. I am deeply grateful for their insightful stewardship and guidance throughout the writing of this book.

Finally, I want to thank my family and dear friends for their support, enthusiasm, and love, especially my mother, Louise; all my "sisters"; my sons, Ransom and Winward; and their beautiful women, Alexandra and Stephanie. Life is rich, indeed. And full of surprises, isn't it?

Introduction: Writing Partnerships

Douglas (1972) writes, "our first concern must be the mechanisms in school by which we deprive children of initiative, of a sense of their own value and potency, of their natural, self-determined desire to learn" (18). As educators, we must be deeply concerned with student initiative, searching, always, for strategies to encourage learners' active engagement. One means of fostering student initiative, then growing and keeping it is by providing writers with opportunities for co-composing. This book describes writing partnerships and the many ways these collaborative relationships support and encourage K through 5 writers as they take the lead to develop independent writing strategies and skills by working together.

◾ Seth's Writers

First graders Leo and Brian sit face-to-face on chairs, clipboards resting on their knees. Their teacher, Seth Paster, has just taught a minilesson on "showing, not telling" and these writers are revising a story so that they "show" instead of "tell."

Leo	Brian
[*writes*] *fluffy*	Yeah!
[*writes*] *His big fluffy jacket*	
	and his . . .
[*writes*] *and his* [*points, rereads*]	
	his big heavy backpack

[*writes*] *his big heavy backpack?*
[*rereads*] He was on the school bus
[*looks up at Brian, then writes*]
and he went [*looks at Brian*]

No! In the big bus!

[*writes*] *on the bus?*

big bus?

How about huge?

These writers continue, mostly "telling" not showing, but their collaboration excites and energizes each as they work hard on their revision—not always a popular task for primary-grade writers. As they complete their work, their mutual satisfaction is evident.

Leo
Yeah!

Brian

We made this story much better

Yeah, with our ideas.

We have good ideas.

Let's go show Mr. Paster.

■ Partnerships for Writing: Why Use Them?

If we regard curriculum as shaping what's already there (Rose 1989), writing partnerships allow this shaping to occur through children's active involvement in every facet of the writing process. Texts created during joint composing incorporate the voice, expertise, and experience of both authors and result in unique compositions that are often more sophisticated and complex than those the writers would compose alone. Just as reading partnerships help children make the transition from shared and guided reading to completely independent reading (Griffin 2001, 2002; Prescott-Griffin 2004, 2005a, 2005b; MacGillivray 1997; MacGillivray and Hawes 1994), writing partnerships provide a bridge between shared, modeled, and interactive writing and the sometimes daunting task of solo composing (Cicalese 2003; Wiseman 2003). Writing partnerships allow children to apply strategies learned during direct instruction while observing and incorporating the ideas and strategies of others into their literate repertoire (Condon and Clyde 1996). When working together, peers scaffold each other's literacy learning in myriad ways, through discussion, assisting behaviors, and modeling (Griffin 2002).

For many primary-grade children, the solitary act of writing can be overwhelming—forming letters, matching sounds and symbols, choosing topics and content, maintaining interest and attention. For upper-elementary-age students, writing not only presents many of the same challenges but also adds increased demands for organization, revision, and genre specific writing. When working with a partner—talking, sharing ideas, and even jointly composing—the task of writing is often more enjoyable so collaborators can support each other's engagement with literate tasks for longer, more sustained periods (Condon and Clyde 1996; Griffin 2001, 2002; Prescott-Griffin 2004, 2005a, 2005b; MacGillivray 1997; MacGillivray and Hawes 1994; Tharp and Gallimore 1988; Wertsch 1985; Wiseman 2003).

The concept of co-authoring and composing through conversation is supported by constructivist theories of learning (Fosnot 1996; Barnes 1992, 1995; Cook-Gumperz 1986; Dewey 1938; Piaget 1976), where learners actively construct knowledge through discussion, problem solving, and joint exploration. For Vygotsky (1978) and other social constructivists, "learning is not viewed from the perspective of the individual, but in terms of the interaction of the individual with others" (Griffin 2001, 375). For them, knowledge is not in the world to be absorbed, nor is knowledge in our brains waiting to be awakened. Rather, it is generated and constructed by humans acting in the world" (Steward 1995, 16).

Dewey (1938) believed that children learn about themselves—who they are and how they learn—through collaboration with others. In stating their belief about learning, Van Der Veer and Valsiner (1993) claim, "Speech is not only a tool of communication, but also a tool of thinking, consciousness [developing] mainly with the help of speech and [originating] in social experience" (64). Talk and social interaction are, therefore, critical for students' learning at all levels, K through 5. Interaction with peers stimulates writers, encourages and prompts their nascent literate efforts, and helps them develop more positive perceptions about writing and "a more creative, free style of written expression" (Cicalese 2003, 36). Language becomes a powerful force as children confer in shared literacy contexts (Griffin 2001). Literacy learning, supported through teacher instruction, is scaffolded through peer-to-peer interactions (Wiseman 2003), and collaboration builds the strategies that young writers may later use independently.

No matter how teachers choose to use writing partnerships, these collaborations support the writing development of all kinds of learners. English language learners and native speakers of every ability level need many opportunities to write with role models available to them. They also need time and space to experiment with language, to make mistakes, and to take risks in a safe, secure environment (Hadaway 1990).

Even when the writing pieces children create are "only marginally successful, the process [of joint composing] provides opportunities for co-authors to observe and adopt the strategies others use" (Condon and Clyde 1996, 586). As partners work together, the shifting nature of assistance is apparent (Tharp and Gallimore 1988) as they deepen their understandings about the composing process for use later in independent writing. When working in literate relationships with peers who are closest to them in development, children learn what works and what does not (Griffin 2002).

This book supports the role of the explicit teacher, who models and provides direct instruction of the skills, strategies, and concepts writers need while exploring ways that children can teach educators about teaching. As teacher Sharon Roberts says

> I saw partner writing as a way for me to step out of the lead role of carrying on those conversations I'd been having [during interactive writing] and now they do them [the conversations] with their partners. So, when they're reminding their partner of a grammatical feature or practicing a strategy like rereading to make sure it [their writing] makes sense . . . or they're using the word wall as a tool, they're carrying on independently. It [partner writing] took me out of the role of guiding them through . . . and now they're doing it with their partner. I think the conversations and the child-to-child teaching that go along with partner writing are as valuable as the writing that takes place.

The variety of co-authoring structures provided here illustrates the many ways that K through 5 teachers can incorporate writing partnerships into existing literacy programs. Just as children collaborate for reading (Prescott-Griffin 2005a, 2005b), they also put their heads together over writing. Observing writers in partnership shows a great deal about the social nature of literacy. Teachers, therefore, are encouraged to pay close attention to what co-authoring interactions reveal about student-initiated teaching strategies as well as learners' interests and motivation. Such observations help educators to better scaffold children's writing "where they are" and to more effectively plan instruction for all learners.

Writing with a partner is fun and gives students opportunities to teach each other while jointly composing text of all kinds. Partners laugh over their inventions, discuss story lines, puzzle over how to incorporate information gleaned through joint research, confer, and problem solve at all stages of writing, from first drafts through multiple revisions. As teachers consider implementing writing partnerships, questions arise:

- Where do writing partnerships fit in my already-crowded literacy program?
- How can writing partnerships support what I'm doing?
- What makes a compatible partner?

- What criteria should we use in pairing students?
- What kinds of writing are best suited to co-composing?
- What models of co-composing support students' genre composition?
- How can I adapt writing partnerships to support *all* students?

The strategies and ideas that follow assist teachers in incorporating writing partnerships that strengthen and support what they are *already doing*. Chapters in Part One provide a rationale for using writing partnerships and give specific suggestions for implementing and supporting these collaborations in both primary and intermediate grades. The chapters in Parts Two and Three explore a variety of writing models to use with writing partnerships and small, collaborative groups of writers.

There are many variations on writing partnerships; each with something to offer developing writers. The procedures and steps in Parts Two and Three are jumping-off points. Teachers can select strategies that serve their students and classroom programs and adapt them accordingly. Writing collaboration takes many forms. Two or more writers may share the pen and jointly compose text, or they may act as research buddies working side by side and assisting each other with reading, note taking and multiple drafts of writing pieces. Writing collaborators may act as responders or editors for one another in one-on-one partnerships or small groups. Sometimes partners correspond, carrying on written conversations about their reading or classroom studies. Writing partnerships also thrive in buddy-writing centers and at home, where children collaborate with parents, caregivers, or siblings. Whatever the context, teacher support and modeling is critical if writing partners are to make effective use of this time.

■ English Language Learners

All learners benefit when teachers structure time for joint composing, provide support and guidance, and invite writers to share their successes and frustrations.

Co-authoring is particularly supportive of learners of English because this strategy provides children with collaborative, nurturing literacy contexts in which to practice skills taught during direct instruction. While Chapter 5 explores in detail the value of writing partnerships for English language learners, each strategy chapter also includes a specific discussion about ELL strategies and adaptations.

■ Concluding Thoughts

Since many real-life writing projects require collaboration, we want to encourage collaboration in young writers as they move toward independence.

Just as we aim to foster our students' critical, active reading, we also want to support them as they grow into strong, competent, independent writers who take responsibility for all phases of the composition process—from generating ideas, taking notes, and writing "sloppy copies" to final revisions and publishing for an audience. In recognition of this goal, each chapter in Parts Two and Three also includes a discussion of extending the strategy into writers' independent work.

1 | Implementing Writing Partnerships

When creating and implementing writing partnerships, teachers draw on many elements of cooperative learning (Kagan 1992) to provide multi-structural lessons that build on one another and move students through learning experiences according to teachers' learning objectives and curricular focus. Depending on students' age and development, writing collaborations will vary considerably from grade to grade and classroom to classroom, but teachers continue to have clear objectives and expectations for these cooperative, collaborative interactions. In the snapshots that follow, first graders and fourth graders are working as "research buddies." The partnership model of Research Buddies is described in greater detail in Chapter 15.

■ Betsy and Hannah: Primary Partnerships in Action

While first graders, Betsy and Hannah begin the year as strong, confident developing readers; they approach writing and writers workshop more tentatively, with less confidence and enthusiasm. Responsible and conscientious, they each understand expectations—during writers workshop, they write. Yet, despite diligence and responsibility, each writer struggles in her own way, written work brief with little liveliness or descriptive detail. Clearly, neither writer is working to her potential. Every writing time, Betsy pens two- to three-sentence stories telling about something she likes to do or sometimes recounting a recent event in her life and no amount of encouragement or cajoling on my part will induce her to elaborate. Then, there is Hannah, who recognizes the importance of filling the page, and fill it she does, writing daily renditions of "I Love" stories. Her journal pages are filled with "I love my mommy, I love my daddy, I love my kitty, I love my grandma."

In all literacy work—read-alouds, shared reading, guided and independent reading and writing—I emphasize collaboration and building knowledge together. In every subject area, we share our thinking through interaction. From the first day of school, children have had reading buddies, as these collaborations are a foundational aspect of my literacy program. However, although I encourage children to talk and confer during the planning phases of writers workshop, composing, up to now, has been a solitary endeavor. By early November, a number of writers are floundering, unable to generate or commit to topics. Despite encouragement and instruction, their stories are often short, lifeless, and rote. While whole-class minilessons provide writers with daily shots in the arm and we frequently brainstorm and share ideas for writing topics, I decide I need to go further and I begin encouraging children to find writing buddies.

One morning, Betsy and Hannah sit down at a table to discuss possible joint writing ideas. As I pass by, they explain that they are having difficulty in agreeing on a mutually interesting topic. They ask me for ideas and I suggest they take a stroll around the classroom to see if anything leaps out as a topic or phenomena they might like to research and write about. Several minutes later, I observe them rushing back to their table, scrambling to find pencils and papers. Curious to discover what has caused such excitement, I check in. Eyes ablaze, they tell me they are going to write a story about Jessie, our much-beloved classroom ferret. Betsy is one of Jessie's chief caretakers, among the few children able to hold him firmly and calmly while others pet him. Hannah loves Jessie, but keeps her distance, preferring to admire him from afar. Eagerly, they set to work, each taking a turn as scribe. By the end of writers' workshop, they have created the following story:

Jessei

Jessei sleeps all Day and night. he loves to play with children. his mother is our techer Mrs. Griffin. he is blake and Brownish wite. He got mared to Sniffils. I like Jessie. I held Jesie at the weding.

dududud ["The Wedding March"]
dududdududu ["The Wedding March"]

he is 20 in's log and [has] a small nose. He had ants all over his cage. we moved iT To The shellf.

During sharing time, the girls sit side by side in the Author's Chair and deliver a spirited choral reading of their collaborative story. They receive much applause, many questions, and several suggestions for adding to their story—in particular details about the ferret wedding. This event was suggested, planned, and staged by the children the previous week, resulting in Jessie's betrothal to Sniffles, a female ferret belonging to one of my students. In preparation for the wedding, the children sewed a wedding gown for Sniffles and mini tuxedo for Jessie during our twice-weekly afternoon activity periods. They also assigned each person a role. There was a pastor (nondenominational) and a large number of flower girls who strew paper rose petals from frilly baskets. Someone also acted as the organ, hence the *dududdud* of the "The Wedding March."

After thanking their audience, the girls take their places in the circle, firm plans for revision in hand. During subsequent writers workshops, Betsy and Hannah revise and expand their story into a small booklet about Jessie, with one chapter devoted solely to the wedding. Following this collaboration, they return to independent writing, but occasionally collaborate with each other or different partners during various phases of the writing process. Like many of their classmates, some of their independent pieces are well developed, others less so, but I am convinced that their time collaborating was instrumental in encouraging and supporting their development as solo writers at a critical juncture in their development in ways independent writing could not. The experience of writing with a buddy on a topic about which they both felt passionate, coupled with the continuous sharing of ideas and strategies, motivated each individual. I also believe that these writers persisted with their joint writing task much longer than each would have done alone.

Betsy and Hannah's playful collaboration can be likened to the interactions in which many adult writers engage daily. In the heat of collaboration, ideas are continualy tossed around, accepted, rejected, and altered. In the partnership context, concerns about right, wrong, good enough, or other forms of censorship are absent. This allows each individual to take isks, experiment, and, in the process, develop competencies she will later use independently.

Through her work with Betsy, Hannah gained the confidence to let go of the "I Love" format and investigate new and compelling topics. Betsy learned to accept feedback on her writing without collapsing emotionally. Prior to this collaboration, Betsy had regarded suggestions from her peers or me as intrusive. Like many first graders, once she committed something to paper, she saw no need to revise, change, or elaborate on stories. With a partner beside her in the Author's Chair, however, Betsy was more receptive and accepting of suggestions for revision. In fact, following this experience, Betsy seemed to find the entire process of revision—particularly when adding details to the wedding chapter—fun and exhilarating. This excitement about revision is rare in young writers and for Betsy it carried over into her willingness to rework individual writing pieces.

■ Intermediate Writing Partnerships in Action

Cindy Pasieka's fourth graders are seated at their desks, which are arranged in clusters of four. Each cluster consists of two writing partnerships. Cindy intentionally pairs writers who are compatible socially and who she believes will support and assist each other as equal partners, rather than partnerships where one writer usurps the task from the other. At Cindy's request, students have brought their language arts journals with them when they changed seats to join their "writing group." Partners sit side by side, opposite the other set of partners.

At present, Cindy's fourth grade is studying Native Americans. Today's task, as Cindy explains it, will be to reread an article on Native Americans on which they read and took notes the previous day. After rereading they will work together to write a paragraph summarizing their article. For this work, Cindy refers writers to their T-A-S-K guidelines posted on an easel (Figure 1–1). Writers at all grade levels in this K through 5 elementary school use this structure.

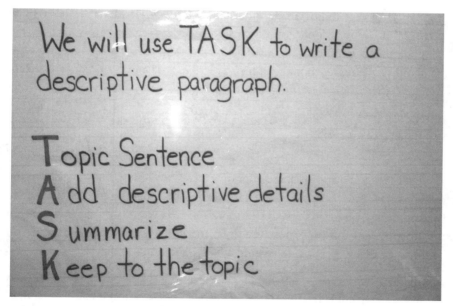

We will use TASK to write a descriptive paragraph.

Topic Sentence
Add descriptive details
Summarize
Keep to the topic

FIG. 1–1   *T-A-S-K Chart*

T-A-S-K is a writing organization strategy developed and used in Cindy's school district of St. James, New York. The structure is as follows:

- **T**opic sentence
- **A**dd descriptive details
- **S**ummarize
- **K**eep to the topic

Cindy reminds partners of the sentence they created the day before. As she repeats the sentence aloud, she writes it on the whiteboard. *First the Iroquois used elm tree trunks to build the frame.* Cindy has dual objectives for this activity: a process focus—using transition words in writing; and a content focus—identifing resources that Native Americans used for building. Cindy says, "You'll be writing a paragraph about how your shelter was built." She reminds them about the importance of accurate sequencing, logical transitions, and the use of sequence words like "first." Then she tapes a long list of transition words to the bottom of the whiteboard. This list is also available to students in their writing notebooks. She adds, "Be sure to use many transition words in your paragraph. That is your job."

Cindy tells writers to be sure to include in their paragraph the resources Native Americans used to build the shelters. Finally, she reminds them about using a topic sentence to "grab the attention of the reader"; reviews the steps for writing a summary; and emphasizes the importance of ending their paragraph with a concluding or summarizing sentence. These skills have been taught in previous lessons, and Cindy simply reviews them here.

As writers begin, I check in with Hally and Gail, who are reading and writing about wigwams, each taking a turn as scribe. Sara and Annie sit across from them and they, too, are writing about wigwams.

Hally	**Gail**
Hey, maybe we should use . . . ?	(*offers a suggestion*)
(*points to their notes*)	

The girls continue to point and confer quietly as they study their notes from the previous day. Their discussion is characterized by much tentative talk, where they point, ask questions, make short, one- or two-word comments, and listen for the other's response. Across the desk, the other pair, Annie and Sara, also converse in this way, actively writing at the same time.

Annie	**Sara**
Let's find a transition word	
[*leafs through her journal*]	

They have a short discussion about the use of commas.

I use . . . [*points to comma*]

After . . . after that, the other trees
[*gestures a wrapping motion
   with her hands*]
. . . wrap around the wigwam.

As Sara writes, Annie continues to consult the article and their notes.

[*writes a sentence, then pushes paper
to Annie*] Your turn!

I was looking while you were
  doing that
[*shows Sara the article*] then finally . . .

Annie gestures, repeats information, and rehearses what she will write. At this point, Hally leans across the table and says, "We missed something so we had to go back to them." Cindy checks in briefly with both pairs, then moves on.

Gail	**Hally**
[*writes sentence Hally has dictated, then pushes the paper to her*]	
	[*writes*] *They used fieldstones to build a fireplace.* But it wasn't really a fireplace. It was just a fire. Want me to read it over?
[*nods*]	
	[*rereads paragraph*] But what did they use? They used bark on the outside.

Hally and Gail study the article. Then, Gail writes another thought about the "long house." Following this, Hally holds up their paragraph, showing it to Sara and Annie, asking, "How'd you like it?"

Between periods of writing, the four girls continue to use tentative, "thinking talk," consulting their partners and talking across partnerships. They also consult the original article and their notes. Their talk is punctuated by frequent pauses where writers stop to think, and there are many "hmms," "likes," and truncated talk as they brainstorm what they know about wigwams from their reading and life experiences, then plan and make decisions about what they will write.

Much is going on in this short writing activity—one of the many times Cindy incorporates writing partnerships into her literacy program. Children of all ages "discover how to learn through talk" (Wells 1986, 65). The importance of talk at every stage of the writing process has been well documented (Calkins 1994; Graves 1983). The tentative, "thinking talk" (Barnes 1992) in which these four writers engage serves many functions for composers as they play with ideas, discard them, stop to think, consult resources (text, their notes, writing journals), consult their partner, and check in across partnerships. Having a collaborator or small group of collaborators provides these writers with access to many modes of thinking and perspectives not so readily available when working alone. Summarizing is a difficult skill for any writer. Collaboration enables all writers to engage in this challenging task aided by supportive conversation and access to one another's thinking.

Cindy has created clear frameworks and structures for her writing partnerships. Each participant knows her role and all writers feel comfortable taking risks and engaging in playful, idea-generating talk as they work together to complete their task. Some of Cindy's rules and structures for partners are:

- Partners sit side by side.
- Each partner writes.
- Both partners contribute ideas no matter who holds the pen.
- Partners reread their writing frequently.

■ Classroom Context

Classroom *communities* are characterized by open communication between all participants. Both Cindy's fourth-grade and my first-grade communities are people oriented. Each member is encouraged to support, trust, and work alongside peers; to take risks; and to problem solve through active involvement in class activities. Each literacy program is balanced and comprehensive and includes time for reading aloud, shared and guided reading and writing, and group and individual work. Cindy formally makes use of mentor texts in her writing program while I use such materials in a more informal way. Mentor texts are short pieces of exemplary literature (usually picture books), or segments of any kind of text that teachers use as models. Mentor texts are read and reread to young writers in order to highlight elements of style, process, voice, and structure that are explicitly taught during writing workshop (Davis and Hill, 2003). In each of these classroom settings, both reading and writing partnerships thrive. Over the years, I have observed teachers partnering children for writing in a wide range of classroom contexts using any number of models and structures for these collaborations. Some questions teachers should ask themselves, when considering writing partnerships are:

- Who should make pairing decisions—the teacher or the students?
- What kinds of supports and structures do writing partners need to be successful?
- What types of writing collaborations will benefit my students?
- What should I consider when supporting writers in all genres of text?

■ Minilessons to Get Writing Partnerships Started

When introducing writing partnerships, most teachers provide minimal guidelines: for example, first-grade teacher Sharon Roberts tells her students, "choose a topic from your experience, share and discuss, figure out how you will share the pen, then get started." Later, as partnerships take off, more formal minilessons and whole-class brainstorming sessions focus on strategies for successful partnerships. Students also tell us which kinds of structures and strategies work for them. Third grader Meg describes why she and her partner take turns, each writing two sentences: "If we [switched roles] every paragraph, we might get mixed up . . . and, well . . . some people might write more than other people because they have more ideas. But we write two sentences at a time and it works for us." Beginning minilessons might include discussion or instructions about the following:

1. *How to share the writing.* Who holds the pen? When should writers alternate the writing task? Sentence by sentence? Paragraph by paragraph? Page by page? What are other roles for writers besides actually writing? Some of the ways students share the writing are:
   - Each writes a word, or a few words.
   - Each writes a sentence, or a few sentences.
   - Each writes a "whole thought."
   - Each writes a paragraph, then switches.
   - One writes and one thinks.
   - In a triad, one person writes, another is the resource person, and the third is the magic-tape person (who applies correction tape when revising).

2. *Expectations for the writing task.* Are there length requirements? Teachers may provide outline formats, graphic organizers, or other planning and organizational tools for writing partners.

3. *Seating arrangements.* Should partners sit side by side? Opposite one another? In Cindy's lesson, seating is defined—partners sit side by side, opposite another partnership. While I usually specify that reading partners must sit side by side, I usually allow writing partners more latitude in choosing how and where they will sit in relation to one another.

4. *What to do if a problem arises.* As much as we try to organize students into compatible partnerships, these interactions are sometimes quite challenging for students, particularly reluctant, self-conscious writers. Modeling scenarios where problems arise and are solved by partners can be helpful for everyone.

5. *Materials and resources.* Writers of all ages love tools, and we want to be sure to provide them with the tools they need for whatever genre they are composing. We also want to teach them how to locate and use appropriate resources and materials. Finally, we want to discover from *them*, what kinds of tools they have created or found to be particularly helpful and supportive.

Effective partnerships do not just happen, nor do they always sustain themselves in isolation. Collaborators need support, guidance, and clear ideas about what is expected of them during joint composing. As time goes on and they become comfortable working together, minilessons and whole-class gatherings can incorporate student sharing and modeling of what works for their partnership.

■ Pairing Decisions

Pairing is about listening to children and getting to know their academic, social, and emotional needs. If we want to pair children compatibly for reading, writing, or any academic work, we must learn about their passions and interests, their likes and dislikes, their preferences and friendships. Sometimes friends make excellent partners, sometimes they don't. Sometimes partnerships create friendships, sometimes they don't (Prescott-Griffin 2005a).

Condon and Clyde (1996) found that, generally, the most successful co-authoring relationships are ones where students choose their own partners or small groups, thereby "building upon already established relationships" (593). In my primary-grade classroom and many other K through 5 classrooms where I have observed, successful partnerships evolve in a variety of ways. Some teachers, myself included, make pairing decisions based on knowledge of learners' interests, abilities, and working preferences. Others provide guidance, structure, and modeling, then let students choose and organize their own writing relationships. Still others alternate between teacher pairing and student selection.

Daniels and Bizar (1998) write that "cooperation requires structure" as well as regular routines, rules, and procedures so that "working together is not a disruptive departure but rather business as usual" (63). No matter who makes

pairing decisions about writing partnerships, it is important to establish a structure, with students about what makes a good partner and an effective writing partnership. Providing whole-class discussion time for children to share successful collaborative strategies helps everyone make the most of these relationships. Equally important is allowing space and discussion time for partners to share frustrations and behaviors that may interfere with effective writing collaborations.

In pairing writers, teachers consider many factors—social and academic compatibility, gender, expertise, interests and experiences. Once partnerships are formed, teachers must consider how long they will remain together and what kinds of writing activities on which they will expect children to collaborate. Depending on the task and requirements, teachers may want to give students the option to work together or alone.

When creating effective writing partnerships, I prefer pairing students of approximately equal expertise. Equal expertise does not mean the same expertise, as each partner brings his own individual experience to the writing. When writers are with peers, however, there is less chance of one usurping the task from the other and more opportunity to put heads together and problem solve over text.

How Long Will Partners Stay Together?

British primary teacher Emma Smith usually makes the decisions about partnerships for her third-year students, eight- and nine-year-olds, but likes to keep groupings flexible and often changes writing partnerships daily, depending on writing tasks and expectations. Other teachers pair children spontaneously when a lesson or activity lends itself to collaboration. If we want children to develop mutually supportive relationships, however, we may also want to consider establishing partnerships that remain together for longer periods of time. Children need time to develop and structure collaborative relationships. In many K through 5 classrooms, my own included, writing partners remain together for a sustained period of time unless children are experiencing difficulties. In my first grade, writing buddies stay together for six to eight weeks. In other classrooms, teachers change partnerships weekly, monthly, or every few months. Teachers conference with writers, present minilessons, and facilitate brainstorming sessions focused on strategies for writing collaboratively. During that time, partnerships may join together for a period or shift and change slightly. By and large, however, they remain together, building and strengthening their literate relationships.

While I assign pairs, some teachers allow writers to choose partners. Others give students choice as to whether to partner at all.

Pairing for Subject, Task, and Expectation

Students who are at different stages of development may still be at a similar level in terms of problem solving. Therefore, as teachers use partnerships across the curriculum, they make a variety of decisions about pairing depending on subject, task, and expectations. During math, cross-ability pairing allows all children to be successful and participate fully during explorations and investigative activities. Cross-age or cross-ability partnerships (see Chapter 3) allow more experienced writers to assist developing writers in a variety of tasks, from research and gathering information to composing, editing, and revision.

Teacher Sharon Roberts uses a variety of partnerships, depending on the task, expectations and needs of her students. In forming writing partnerships with her first graders, she uses a "color buddies" system. These pairings change every four to six weeks. Her color buddies partnerships begin midway through the year, but teachers may begin much earlier depending on their programs and students.

In the color buddies system, each child is paired in four different ways:

1. Red Buddy = child's choice
2. Green buddy = Sharon's choice (according to skill or ability level, social needs, etc.)
3. Blue buddy = by gender (boy–girl partnerships)
4. Orange buddy = by reading level (the child is usually paired with a compatible member of his or her guided reading group).

Teachers are encouraged to remain flexible in creating writing partnerships for different writing genres, paying close attention to children's interests, experiences, and background in a subject. Certain writers love dialoguing with peers, while others are more reticent. Some children love the challenge of research and gathering information while others need more guidance and structure. Christine Mikalyzk pairs her fifth-grade students very deliberately in preparation for her monthlong biography-writing project in order to support the number of special needs students in her fifth-grade classroom. (For a description of this project and Christine's decisions about pairing, see Chapters 6 and 15.)

No matter how teachers pair readers, or for how long, they need to respect what students are telling them about what works and what does not. "If learning is thinking" (Daniels and Bizar 1998, 64), then we want to remember that students will thrive and grow in *compatible relationships* that teach them how to think. Third grader Sally says it best, in relating to me how she and her partner begin to co-compose.

Mary Lee	**Sally**
How do you and your partner get started . . . get organized?	
	Um . . . we figure out what's good for both of us.
And how do you figure that out?	
	Well, we both have to decide on one thing and . . . well, one of us says something, we know each other so . . . the other one thinks and decides if it's good for them.

■ Challenges and Conflict Resolution

No matter how carefully teachers pair children, taking into account academic, social, and emotional factors, some writers find collaboration extremely challenging. The most common issues for writing buddies center on ownership of the task and decision making about what to write and how to do it. Other issues arise when reluctant, self-conscious writers feel uncomfortable in the presence of a more capable, engaged peer. Even when children are closely matched in their expertise and motivation, one partner may perceive herself to be less competent and, as a consequence, take a more passive or disengaged role.

When I observe partners struggling with issues of ownership and control of task, I sometimes sit in briefly, then suggest structures that are more equal. I might also ask them to join another partnership where writers are working collaboratively and, for a few days, be a "partnership of four." In this way, their peers model and share strategies and behaviors they can take back to their twosome.

If partners' issues center around conflict, Thomas Gordon's (2000) book *Parent Effectiveness Training* can be helpful—especially his six-step process for conflict management. Although Gordon's book is aimed at parents, his six steps provide a clear framework that is easy to share with writing or reading partners wrestling with issues of power, control, choice, decision making, and ineffective communication. Basically, the six steps are:

1. Identify the source of conflict.
2. Brainstorm possible solutions.

3. Discuss each possible solution.
4. Select the best solution and tell each other why it's best.
5. Develop a plan to carry out the solution.
6. Put the solution into practice, discuss how it's going, and change or modify it as necessary.

My first graders are able to understand these steps and, as experienced brainstormers, take to the process readily. Since step four may spark a struggle for control during decision making, some partnerships require a third party to sit in. Usually I find that my intervention—in the form of listening and asking questions—is often enough to remind children of the previous steps and their good and fruitful discussions about all possible solutions. If, after my intervention, they are still unable to agree on the "best solution," I tell them each to choose one and write it on a slip of paper, then we draw one from a hat.

2 | Small-Group Writing Collaborations

Partners help you get information and when you're stuck, they help you write on!

—Second grader

■ Small-Group Writing Collaborations: What Are They?

The exchange of many voices and ideas during small-group collaborations may work better for some writers as an alternative to the sometimes more intensive, one-on-one partnerships. In this model, groups of four or five students come together to collaborate over a piece, or pieces, of writing. Groups can be teacher-created or formed when a cluster of students share a common interest or passion.

Small groups have a number of benefits for writers. First, writers receive the support and assistance of many peers. Second, they profit from the enthusiasm and active participation of others, as they share ideas, skills, and strategies. Third, from a practical standpoint, small-group writing collaborations allow a sharing of resources—print and media—particularly when writers all want to make use of the same materials on a subject at the same time. Small-group collaborative writing mimics what many adults do every day—collaborate and jointly

create—and, is, therefore, a great rehearsal for real-world tasks. In these collaborative contexts, writers develop lifelong skills and strategies extending far beyond classroom walls.

■ Strategy in Action

Kristine Kefor's third graders are collaborating to write summaries of their work comparing and contrasting characters from a story they have recently read. Three girls work together, taking turns writing, finding resources, and leading the discussion. They are experienced collaborators and waste little time on organizational routines that are, at this point, well established. No matter who holds the marker, all three students contribute ideas to the summary. Every few minutes, they pause as one writer holds up the large paper copy of their story that they reread chorally, either editing and revising or going on.

■ Getting Started: Guidelines and Models for Small-Group Writing Collaborations

While small-group writing collaborations may be more suited to writers in grades 2 through 5, teachers of younger children often incorporate small-group work into their literacy programs. My first graders love to work in groups to compose the letters, stories, charts, newsletters, and create posters. They also enjoy collaborating on illustrations for whole-group interactive writing pieces.

As with any type of writing partnership, it is not enough to group children and sit back. No matter what age the children or what model used, it is critical that teachers provide explicit instruction—modeling, demonstrating, teaching, and reteaching guidelines, structures, and expectations for small-group writing collaborations. It is also crucial to provide time for groups to share their experiences so that writers can benefit from one another's wisdom. Considerations when implementing collaborative writing groups are:

- establishing community and trust
- developing minilessons to support small-group collaborations
- grouping students to support each individual

Establishing Community and Trust

Community and trust are critical elements when asking children to share tentative, often very rough drafts of their writing. Writers need to know, without question, that peers in their writing group are there *to support and encourage them*, just as the teacher is. Building a sense of community and trust is often *the curriculum* for the first four to six weeks of school as teachers and students negotiate and establish classroom rules, define routines for each day, institute procedures and steps for academic tasks, and come to know each other.

No matter how many years students remain together, the first day of a new school year is the first time they meet as fourth or fifth graders. Thus, they meet each year in new roles and need to rebuild a sense of community and trust. A few ways for teachers to create, maintain, and deepen a sense of community and trust in classrooms are:

- Invite students to share in creating classroom rules.
- Invite students to share in establishing classroom routines and rituals.
- Invite students to help define and organize classroom spaces and room arrangement.
- Invite students' input and suggestions about curriculum, classroom projects, and areas of study.
- Establish a daily "circle time" where students greet each other, share stories from their lives, and exchange ideas and knowledge.
- Cede responsibility to students for familiar teaching tasks, such as "word of the day."

Time to Share   Just as we close readers and writers workshops with sharing, writing groups need to come together with the whole class at the end of a writing session to share their experiences, their successes, and their frustrations. This is an excellent time to establish trust, learn about each other, and celebrate individual accomplishments.

Developing Minilessons to Support Small-Group Collaborations

Teachers will want to plan minilessons tailored to needs of their students and curriculum, but general areas of importance to small groups of writers may be:

- teacher and student modeling
- teacher and student scaffolding
- creating rules for writing groups

Teacher and Student Modeling   Before sending groups off to work together, teachers make expectations clear. They also model supportive, assisting behaviors, and introduce writers to the "language of response" (Brady and Jacobs 1994). Both teachers and students can be wonderful models of supportive assistance, with teachers starting off, then releasing responsibility to students. With time and space to share and model experiences, learners develop effective strategies teachers may never have thought to suggest. Group members can share experiences through:

- *talk*—The group simply tells about their work, or
- *"fishbowl"-demonstrations*—one group sits at the front of the classroom or in the middle of other class members and demonstrates how they work. The rest of the class observes, then shares what they notice after the demonstration.

Teacher and Student Scaffolding   Wood, Bruner, and Ross (1976) first used the term *scaffolding* to define the *teacher role* in assisting learning. Like the scaffolding builders use in construction, scaffolding is a temporary kind of help that is withdrawn when the learner no longer needs it. For example, the teacher may sit with groups as they get started, then check in regularly, asking questions and assisting students with language, procedures, and challenges as needed.

Students also provide important kinds of scaffolding to one another (Prescott-Griffin 2004) when they listen, ask good questions, and make suggestions to the writer. When teachers make the concept of scaffolding clear, students learn to differentiate between the writer and reader and see themselves as "writing teachers" whose role is not to tear down or pull apart writing, but to assist the writer in moving further with the process in a particular piece of writing. Typically, when scaffolding is explained to students—they take to it like ducks to water. Seeing oneself as a scaffolder rather than an all-knowing dispenser of knowledge helps adults and children to sit side by side with writers, offering support as they move to a higher level of skill or understanding.

Creating Rules for Writing Groups   Ideally, rules and procedures are developed *with students*. This helps writers take ownership of and responsibility for smooth, effective group interactions. Rules and procedures will vary depending on the type of work a group undertakes. Once they have been created and writers are familiar with them, these guidelines should be readily available to students—posted on the wall, or handed out to students—and should be revisited at the start of group writing work.

Grouping Students to Support Each Individual

Teachers make grouping decisions based on the makeup of the class each year. Some years, I can group children in partnerships and small groups daily for a wide range of academic endeavors. Other years, the social and academic needs of the class and the individual students necessitate individual or whole-class work. No matter what my class make-up is, I use both reading and writing partnerships as well as math buddies every year, because I view these collaborations as vital bridges between my direct instruction and students' independent performance in reading, writing, and math.

Some general questions teachers may want to ask themselves when forming small writing groups would be:

- *How many students make a group?* My preference is, ideally, four, but no more than five per group. I ask students to sit across from each other, face-to-face.
- *How should students be grouped in terms of ability, gender, ethnicity, etc.?* Most teachers, myself included, prefer to group heterogeneously according to ability, gender, ethnicity, and language of origin. While there may be times when we group homogeneously by any of the criteria listed, in general, I prefer to give children access to different viewpoints, levels of expertise, background experiences, and language competencies. Often, it is my

struggling writers who listen raptly, then ask the most probing, thoughtful questions about content.

- *How long should groups remain together?* Teachers consider many criteria in establishing balanced, supportive writing groups, just as they do in establishing supportive, compatible partnerships. Because it takes time to establish trust and mutuality in group work and time to learn about each other so that the support given is substantive rather than superficial, each group slowly develops routines that make the collaborative process work effectively for those four or five writers. I prefer that students build on this foundation rather than start all over with new buddies. So, while I like to change *writing partnerships* every six to eight weeks to give children access to the support of many peers, if writing, I may keep writing groups together for much longer—in some cases an entire semester or school year—if they are working well.

Four Models of Small-Group Writing Collaborations

While there are many models for small-group writing collaborations, four are described below as starting points. As always, teachers are encouraged to design and choose the models and structures that best suit their students and classrooms.

- Peer response or editing groups
- Research and special interest groups
- Group story composing
- Study groups

One of the strengths of collaborative group work is the division of labor as writers work to jointly create a piece of writing. Each group member may have to complete a particular task independently, then return to share with the group. Or, pairs of writers might splinter off to work collaboratively, then return to share work with group.

Peer Response or Editing Groups

Teacher modeling and instruction for peer response groups focuses on the "language of response" (vocabulary and behaviors writers use as audience and mentors for one another's writing), possible questions, tools, and routines for this work. In helping children to converse like writers, teachers may want to teach terms and vocabulary that define and describe process. Such vocabulary might include:

- introduction or lead
- transition or connection
- word-order problem or syntax problem
- word choice
- main idea or thesis
- supporting details or evidence
- ending or conclusion
- audience

Teachers who consistently model and define academic language for students, expect them to use it. While seemingly appropriate only for older students in grades 3 through 5, I have observed this language use in first-grade classrooms where students' level of strategy language and use of response vocabulary was more highly sophisticated than that of many adults.

Peer response groups offer supportive feedback to one another and positive encouragement to fellow writers. Group members listen carefully then suggest strategies to take the writer further. Expectations for editing or response group work are designed to allow children to share their work and receive supportive, helpful feedback. The simple set of rules below establishes clear routines for group process.

1. The writer reads her piece three times.
2. During the first reading, the audience listens.
3. During the second and third readings, the listeners take notes.
4. Group members then take turns responding, first with positive, then assisting, comments and questions.

When children comment on the writing of others, teachers may want to encourage them to respond in a variety of ways to different aspects of the writing. Teachers can model, teach, and encourage writers to direct their responses to one of these six traits of writing (Spandel 2001):

1. *Content or ideas*. Are there main themes and ideas running through a piece of writing? Often, teachers and students refer to this trait as the "heart of the message."
2. *Organization*. This refers to structure of the writing and how an author's ideas flow or build on one another.
3. *Voice*. The personal, unique voice of the author coming through.

4. *Word choice and vocabulary*. Using the words that most clearly and precisely communicate the message.
5. *Sentence variety/usage*. This trait refers to how the writing flows from the sentences a writer creates.
6. *Mechanics/conventions*. This refers to "correctness," including attention to grammar and spelling.

This is one example of a particular program that serves as a familiar framework in a classroom's writing curriculum. The criteria and kinds of small-group writing responses always depend entirely on the program, curriculum, teacher expectations, and needs of students.

Research and Special Interest Groups

In research and special interest collaborations, writers work together on a mutually agreed-on topic, conducting joint research and co-composing written pieces outlining their findings. Depending on curriculum and teacher expectations, research buddies may:

- select a topic together
- collect information together through observations, explorations, experiments, and reading
- take notes together
- co-compose a report outline
- co-compose the final summary/report. At this stage, writers might also work independently to compose their final report.

Group Story Composing

In group story composing, writers collaborate to write stories together. They meet first to share ideas, divide tasks, and select a topic. Or they might collaborate to co-compose a group response to a writing prompt as practice for state or district writing assessments. The group then decides on the organizational tools they will use to map out their story (graphic organizers, story maps, etc.). See Appendix K for a few examples of organizational tools for story planning. In designing a plan or outline, group members discuss and decide on such elements as tone, characters, setting, and plot.

Once an outline or plan for the story is created, the writing group may choose to compose their story together employing a structure similar to a teacher-facilitated shared writing activity, or the group may divide tasks by role, giving each writer or pair of writers in the group the responsibility for certain aspects of the writing. Here are some possible roles for group story writing:

- *Scribe*. Holds the pen; that is, performs the writing.
- *Illustrator*. Directs the illustration production for a story. This person may—alone or with a partner—be responsible for all illustrations or, more typically, assign responsibility for illustrations to group members, then collect and assemble all artwork.
- *Wordsmith*. Takes responsibility for the story's language, often suggesting alternative vocabulary, checking spelling and meaning, and searching for amazing or interesting words.
- *Director*. Takes responsibility for the overall organization of the project, then joins others in completing tasks as needed.
- *Resource Collector*. Finds appropriate resources—dictionaries, thesauruses, Internet and print sources, spelling dictionaries, etc.—as writers need them.
- *Timekeeper*. Keeps track of group work and ensures there is always time for sharing at the end of group writing time.
- *Summarizer*. Whenever writers share segments of text, the Summarizer gives a short report, recapping the main points she has heard.
- *Editor*. While all group members are responsible for editing and revision, the Editor directs this phase of the writing and may, alone or with a buddy, take charge of redrafting a piece following an editing session.

A teacher can encourage this kind of division of labor and role playing by modeling each role. This helps writers assume the jobs with clear expectations for their behaviors. Obviously, if all or most of the roles described are used in a story writing collaboration, each writer within a group of four or five will assume multiple roles. Roles may also change. For example, all members may take a turn acting as Scribe. Or roles can remain fixed for a certain project, then change with the next. Shifting ensures that all writers have experience with all aspects of the process.

Study Groups

As the name implies, study groups come together to collaborate in order to learn or master new material. Study-group work integrates reading and writing processes through active, spirited conversation. Study-group members may keep a "writer's notebook" individually, or the group may keep a shared notebook to record group responses or keep notes about group activities, plans, and responses during sharing.

Study-group activities continually shift from parallel to shared work. During this time, writers read and explore materials; take notes; and find, record, and share the language of books. Depending on the type of study group, members may:

- swap ideas
- share ongoing pieces of writing
- examine and discuss text structures, then discuss their possible use in their own writing
- meet to share notes
- engage in joint study and debate about topics group has selected or been assigned by the teacher
- create group charts and logs of study findings.

Like all models of group work, study groups provide collaborative contexts where writers talk about process, content, and conventions. Through sharing and discussing writing with peers, writers can bring new perspectives to solo writing.

■ Moving Toward Independence

It is often a much easier, less stressful process to listen and critique the work of others than it is to look critically at one's own work. Once writers have this experience in a group, they return to their own writing with fresh eyes, greater confidence, and enhanced competence. Teachers assist and support writers' move to independence by revisiting strategies and skills practiced during collaboration and remind students of the importance of peer teachers. Then, when individual writers are "stuck" or need assistance, they have a number of "teachers" to whom they can turn for help.

■ Suggestions for English Language Learners

Students learning English need access to strong, literate language models as well as opportunities to talk and share ideas and concepts. If we heterogeneously group children most of the time for collaborative group writing, English language learners can experience this kind of ongoing support and modeling. Additional suggestions would be to provide visual models of all expectations by posting them on the walls and giving individual copies to all writers. Teachers may also want to plan for reteaching time, during which they present expectations and guidelines for group work a second time, allowing time for children to ask questions and practice before joining their writing group. Finally, it is important to check in with groups often, making sure that *all* students are participating.

3 | Cross-Age Writing Buddies

They work together so effortlessly, learning language from the third graders that they will use later on.

—Kindergarten teacher Heather Stonehill, about her students'
collaboration with third-grade buddies

CLASSROOM CHALLENGE

My students help each other, but they really need more teacher support than I can give them.

■ Cross-Age Buddies: What Are They?

As the name implies, cross-age writing partnerships involve younger, less experienced writers working with older, more experienced writers. While peers support each other in many ways, mentors who can model what lies ahead offer assistance of another kind to writers. Vygotsky (1978) described a "zone of proximal development," defined as "the distance between the actual developmental level as determined by independent problem solving and the level of potential development as determined through problem solving under adult guidance or in collaboration with more capable peers" (86). Cross-age or mentor buddies act as teachers, guides, and more capable others, helping younger writers reach higher in their potential level of writing development.

■ Heather and Jeanne's Writers

On a cold, early December morning, Heather Stonehill's kindergartners sit at tables, their body language and the quiet buzz revealing their anticipation as they await their third-grade buddies. Jeanne Hall's third graders arrive, quickly locate their buddies, and take seats beside them. After the children are settled, Heather calls their attention to a planning web about winter, similar to those they constructed previously with their buddies. Heather reviews the concepts depicted on the web and asks children for additional suggestions to fill it out. She then introduces the buddy-writing project for the day—

creating a "winter acrostic poem." Buddies are familiar with this activity, having composed "fall acrostic poems" together several months earlier, so Heather's explanation is brief and focuses on the tools they will use—a single sheet of first-draft paper, then a larger, bifolded paper with a decorative border on which they will write their final draft with one side for a winter illustration.

Chloe and Ramona sit side by side, heads together, as they plan each sentence of their acrostic. Ramona, the third grader, holds the pen, waiting for Chloe's ideas before writing. When I check in, they have already completed the following:

White snows covers the earth
In a sleigh we zoom down the hill
Near the stove we can smell the hot chocolate

They have skipped *T* and are working on *E*.

Ramona	Chloe
(*writes*) *Eating Christmas cookies . . .*	We make ourselves!
(*writes*) *we make ourselves.*	(*nods*)
Want to do *T* now?	

We could start with "The"?	(*nods*) Yup.
So what about after "the"?	The animals hibernate during the cold weather.

(*writes*) *The animals hibernate during the cold weather.*

Together, Chloe and Ramona consult their web for an idea for *R*, pointing and talking quietly.

Ramona	**Chloe**
We could use "run"?	Yup.
Running down a hill?	R . . . r . . . r . . . running . . . riding?
	Riding down a steep . . . icy . . .
	hill . . . no, mountain!

We already used "riding." (*rereads their poem and finds this is not correct*). Okay (*writes*) *Riding down a steep, icy mountain.*

Guidelines and expectations for collaboration, supportive listening, revising, and editing have been communicated to Ramona and her classmates during minilessons in Heather's room and in Jeanne's as well. Clear expectations and specific training are essential to the success of cross-age partnerships whether the mentor buddies are older students or adults.

Jeanne and Heather's buddies meet two or more times each month, sometimes reading, sometimes writing, sometimes working on art, science, or math projects. It is an important time for all students. The older writers sharpen and refine skills as they mentor younger readers and writers, while their younger counterparts acquire skills, language, and strategies from the modeling and support of their more experienced buddies.

■ Planning and Supporting Cross-Age Writing Buddies

In planning cross-age writing partnerships, teachers must find appropriate buddies, decide on regular meeting times for collaborations, provide careful guidelines and structures for buddy work, and choose the kinds of writing for this valuable co-composing time.

Appropriate Cross-Age Buddies

Finding appropriate and willing mentor buddies is usually relatively simple when searching for older students to work with primary-grade writers. Locating

buddies for fifth graders may be somewhat more challenging, but if a middle or upper school is close by, an alliance might be forged. Possible partnerships for cross-age writing buddies include:

- *Students from an older grade in the school or district.* Many schools regularly pair students in younger grades with those in older grades for reading support and other activities. If these kind of partnerships are ongoing and meet regularly, students might make ideal cross-age writing buddies.
- *Adult volunteers.* If there is a definite routine and a set time for cross-age buddy writing, parents or community members can be recruited to serve as mentor writers.
- *Siblings and parents.* If certain projects or writing assignments lend themselves to home support for writers, teachers can send home clear guidelines for such work. More specifics on "home writing partnerships" can be found in Chapter 7.

Meeting Times for Cross-Age Buddies

Regular meeting times that both mentor and developing writers can anticipate and rely on are important. Successful cross-age writing collaborators meet regularly—once or twice a week—for the entire school year. Collaborations take time to develop; writers must learn each other's style, strengths, frustrations, and needs. Trust is also something that takes time to build. Therefore, if partnerships are working well, I recommend that, once established, cross-age buddies remain paired for the entire school year.

Training and Guidance for Mentor Writers

Whenever I use adult volunteers in my classroom to help students with reading, writing, or math, I provide training. Most training consists of one or two hourlong sessions where I explain classroom procedures, expectations, and curriculum before I outline the specific kinds of help volunteers will provide for my students. I, and most teachers with whom I have spoken, also provide this kind of training for cross-age writing tutors. Specific recommendations for mentor buddy training include the following:

- *Provide background about curricular goals and expectations.* This is critical if you want mentors to support, rather than undo, what you're doing.
- In addition to providing overall information about the curriculum, you will want to communicate with mentors about your expectations for content and mechanics

   Content: What kinds of questions should mentors ask the writer in addressing content? It is important to focus on content first, rather than mechanics. This is a major concern when training of cross-age writing buddies.

   Mechanics: When is invented spelling acceptable? At what stage should mentors begin working with buddies on correct spelling? When volunteers come into a class to help with writing, spelling often becomes *the* focus instead of content, writer's intentions, voice, and organization. Teachers should make expectations for mechanics clear, then provide updates and reteaching whenever necessary so that volunteers and cross-age buddies are supporting, rather than subverting curricular goals. Mentors should also be clear about the use of editing and revising checklists and guidelines.

- *Provide materials and tools for mentors.* I give classroom volunteers and mentor writers a pocket folder with written outlines and descriptions of everything we go over during training. That way, they can take the information with them, reread it, and come prepared when they meet with their buddies. Other materials and tools I might include or add to their folders as the year goes on are:

  - lists of revising questions
  - revising suggestions

- editing guidelines or checklists
- graphic organizers
- "no excuse" word lists that my students are expected to spell and use correctly.

Training and Guidance for Younger, "Mentee" Writers

Just as teachers provide guidance for more experienced mentors, they should remember to make their expectations for cross-age partnerships clear to younger, less experienced members of these collaborations. Especially important is the reminder that they are expected to be active, engaged partners. A few things to make clear to younger writers would be:

- expectations for their roles as active, full participants
  - whether they are expected to lead and direct a particular project
  - directions and background information they should give their buddy
  - communicating to their buddy when and where they need help
- expectations for *their participation* in tasks
- the importance of listening and responding thoughtfully
- proper use of all tools and resources.

While one partner may possess skills and expertise that the other does not, teachers should strive to make cross-age partnerships as equal as possible in terms of learner participation.

Kinds of Writing for Cross-Age Buddies

The simple answer when teachers ask what kinds of writing or what stages of writing are best for cross-age buddies is, any kind, any stage. Teachers are encouraged to select projects that serve the needs of their students and curriculum in pairing cross-age collaborators. Some kinds of writing to try with cross-age writing buddies are:

1. *Echo writing.* While I would not recommend this as a steady diet for cross-age writing buddies, it's a great warm-up exercise. See Chapter 8 for detailed instructions on echo writing.

2. *Dialogue journals.* These are great shared writing vehicles for cross-age buddies. They are also a good alternative when teachers cannot find collaborators to physically work together in their school building. Once established, journals can be transported back and forth between buildings as buddies dialogue with each other. Dialogues can be established between buddies about everyday experiences, or texts they both read and discuss. For suggestions related to this kind of reflective writing, see Chapter 9.

3. *Structured Writing.* In addition to the "acrostic poem" activity described earlier in this chapter, many other forms of structured writing adapt easily to cross-age buddy writing. For suggestions about and ideas for structured writing, see Chapters 8 and 12.

4. *Research buddies.* Cross-age buddies can collaborate as research partners at any stage in the writing process to:
   - Read through materials together
   - Take notes
   - Record information on graphic organizers
   - Create an outline or plan for writing
   - Co-compose a first draft together
   - Collaborate on revision and editing.

5. *Story writing.* This is a fun project for cross-age writers. Just as peers help each other to brainstorm ideas about plot, characters, and setting, cross-age writers can work together to plan, draft, and revise stories.

■ Moving Toward Independence

The skills children gain from mentor buddies translate to greater confidence and competence when they work alone. Mentor writers also gain insights into the writing process through these collaborations. One way to make explicit connections for cross-age buddies—or any writing partnership—between collaborative work and their independent projects is to periodically ask them to respond verbally or in writing to How's It Going? queries (see Figure 3–1). For a blank "How's It Going" form that can be used with all kinds of writing partnerships, please see Appendix I.

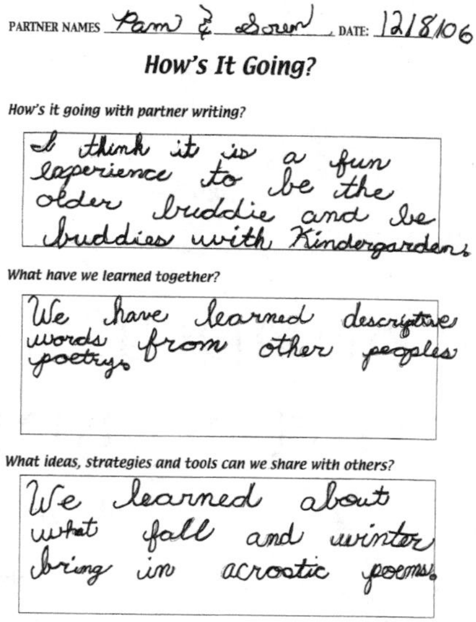

■ Suggestions for English Language Learners

Cross-age partnerships give students learning English valuable modeling and mentoring through the talk, demonstration, and instruction that goes on in these collaborative contexts. When I provide training for mentor writers, I always emphasize the importance of focusing first and foremost on content and the writer and what she is trying to accomplish. This is particularly important for mentor writers working with English language learners, whose struggles with the mechanics and grammar of this second language often obscure the rich content of their message. Astute mentor writers can be helped to look beyond mechanics to the diverse, authentic voices emerging from young writers.

PARTNER NAMES _Pam & Soren_ DATE: _12/8/06_

How's It Going?

How's it going with partner writing?

I think it is a fun experience to be the older buddie and be buddies with Kindergardens

What have we learned together?

We have learned descriptive words from other peoples poetry

What ideas, strategies and tools can we share with others?

We learned about what fall and winter bring in acrostic poems.

FIG. 3–1   "How's It Going?" Chart

4 | Supporting Writing Partnerships

My partner just coached me through this . . . so I can do it on my own in my journal.

—First grader

■ Sharon's Writers

On a late January morning, Sharon Roberts gathers her first graders on the carpet and begins a discussion.

Sharon: Writing and reading are like mirrors of one another and you can make lots of connections between reading and writing. Now, what can you do to help each other?

Child 1: Talk about the story.

Sharon: Yes, talk is really important for writers. It's what they do. And how will you share the writing?

Child 2: My partner writes, then me.

Sharon: Yes, everyone gets a chance to write. And the partner who is not writing needs to pay attention and act as a resource if your partner gets stuck. Now, let's talk about resources. What can you do if your partner gets stuck?

Child 3: Go to the word wall.

Child 4: Clap out the word.

Child 5: Look at the word.

Child 6: Tell 'em . . . or sound it out for them.

Child 7: Look in a book.

Child 8: Ask a teacher. Say, "Where could we go to find the word *play*?"

Child 9: Look at TV.

Sharon: Hmmm . . . we don't have a TV and so what else might we do?

Child 10: If they needed the word *day* that's like *play* and—

Child 11: They could look on the calendar where it says *today*!

Child 12: You could look in your green dictionary.

Sharon: If it's a word wall word, how will you find it?

Child 13: It's highlighted.

Sharon: Yes, it's highlighted.

Child 14: You could look in *The Lady with the Alligator Purse.*

Sharon: Yes, there are lots of places to find words. You can have lots of discussion and talk with your partner about resources—green dictionary, books, word wall. What else is important?

Child 15: Find a good spot to write.

Sharon: Yes, find a spot where you won't be distracted. That's important. Now, can we make a small circle and everyone sit next to their writing buddy?

Sharon Robert's first graders have an hourlong buddy-writing time every Tuesday morning where they compose community messages (see Chapter 13) for other classes, administrators, and teachers in their preschool through grade 3 elementary school. Since students are writing for specific audiences, they pay particular attention to this aspect of their writing, and Sharon is careful during her five-to-eight-minute introductory minilesson/discussion to remind them about audience every week. She also reminds them about the skills they have identified as necessary to be effective collaborators. Finally, Sharon selects a specific instructional focus for each minilesson prior to partner-writing time. Today, her focus is finding resources writers need as they compose. As she does for all her teaching, Sharon carefully structures partner-writing time to give students the tools and support they need to be successful.

■ Supporting Writing Partnerships

Once partnerships are established, there are many ways teachers can help writers to make the most of this valuable collaborative time. The snapshot of

Sharon's classroom illustrates a type of support for writing buddies—the teacher-directed discussion/minilesson—that can be used every time children pair for writing or as often as a teacher deems necessary. Minilessons provide time and space for teacher and student modeling and demonstration, brainstorming ideas, and a forum for writers to share what's working and where they need help during writing partner time. In addition to minilessons, teachers confer with partners, enlist students' ideas for creating visual reminders about collaboration, offer tools and resource materials for partners, and check in to make sure partnerships are running smoothly, intervening when necessary to help children resolve conflicts or challenges.

■ Minilessons and Discussions to Support Collaboration

Minilessons also offer students opportunities "to expand and refine their ideas about composing" (Condon and Clyde 1996). Just as we support children's reading and writing through direct and specific teaching, we support writing partnerships through minilessons focused on strategies for effective collaboration, strategies that support learners' strengths while challenging them to go further. When we model literate behaviors in minilessons, we often perturb writers, contradicting and challenging their views and beliefs about writing (Fosnot 1996). But after such experiences, partners and individuals return to literate tasks with new perspectives with which they examine and modulate their own behaviors (Prescott-Griffin 2005a). Explicit modeling and minilessons provide effective new strategies and tools for children to share, evaluate, and experiment with. In considering how to use minilessons to support writing partnerships, Sharon and her students demonstrate the importance of:

- considering audience
- regularly revisiting skills and strategies for effective collaboration
- regularly reminding writers about independent ways they can help themselves
- having a specific instructional goal or focus for each writing partner time.

Minilessons usually arise from teachers' careful observations of partnerships. They are designed to scaffold writers, taking them from where they are to a higher, more sophisticated level of functioning (Prescott-Griffin 2004). Rowe (1994) suggests that co-authoring experiences transport learners across the zone of proximal development—the distance between a learner's solo performance and what she can achieve when working with more capable others (Vygotsky 1978).

General guidelines for minilessons follow. For ideas on specific aspects of supporting writing partnerships, see the minilessons in each chapter.

- Observe partnerships daily, noting successful behaviors and strategies you want to highlight during minilessons as well as areas where students need guidance and support.
- Keep minilessons short, no more than five to eight minutes.
- Provide space for children to talk, sharing successes and frustrations.
- Make explicit connections between co-authoring activities and other classroom composing such as interactive, shared, and modeled writing; journal writing; and group storytelling.
- Read literature aloud to expose writers to multiple ways of composing.

Modeling: Teachers and Children Sharing "How It's Done"

Some of the most powerful lessons I have observed in support of effective writing collaborations involve modeling or demonstration of some kind. Three types of modeling I have observed are:

1. *Teacher modeling.* The teacher demonstrates or discusses her own writing process or student samples, sharing thoughts, challenges, and successes.
2. *Teacher–student modeling.* The teacher asks a student or two to model an aspect of collaboration with him. See the Strategy in Action section of Chapter 10 for an example of teacher–student modeling.
3. *Student–student modeling.* Students volunteer or a teacher asks a pair of writers to demonstrate or explain some aspect of their collaboration, such as:
   - how they share the pen
   - where they find resources
   - how they get organized for writing
   - how they confer, edit, and respond to each other's writing
   - how they handle difficult or challenging moments.

Modeling demonstrates the collaborative writing process in action; a few minutes of modeling can be worth a thousand words. Frequently, students' modeling has the greatest impact on peers. Teachers are encouraged to observe writing partners often, and to seek partners who can act as "writing teachers" for peers.

Brainstorming and Sharing Ideas That Work

Much of my research centers around discovering what children can teach educators about teaching and which strategies and structures work best for them. When I observe my own students and those in other classrooms, I look for moments of child-to-child teaching. I am continually in awe of the strategies, organizational ideas, and routines children invent when working together. Some of the strategies children have shared with me are:

- how they get organized to begin writing
- how they develop ideas and decide which to use
- how they arrange their "writing area"
- who leads and how this role shifts
- what the listening partner does when not writing
- how they find resources
- tools they develop and use for writing
- how they settle differences and conflict
- how they listen and respond to each other
- how they help the writer to "take another look."

Children are always eager to put their heads together and create procedures that work for them as readers and writers. Providing time for students to share what is working in partnerships gives all writers access to their peers' thinking. This sharing also provides teachers with insights about individual learning styles and preferences, which they can then use to plan instruction and minilessons. Checking in and asking writers to share strategies takes only a few minutes, but yields tremendous wisdom for all.

Extending Partner Talk and Interaction

Talk is a vital part of any writers workshop, whether students are working alone or with partners. Teachers should, therefore, seek many ways to encourage writers' literate talk. Second-grade teacher Cheryl Feeney says, Conferring is at the heart of partners' work. I am always working to encourage all kinds of talk. One thing I often say [in] whole group that reinforces what I hope they'll do on their own is—"Writers, I would like you to go eye to eye, knee to knee for five minutes . . . two minutes . . . however long." I say things like, "partner one, you talk first, then partner two." I try to be very direct and clear.

Once partnerships are established and collaborators are working well together, minilessons can be designed to extend partner talk, focusing in on particular elements in texts they are reading or writing. Teachers also encourage partners to elaborate and converse over individual pieces or co-composing efforts. Here are some areas where teachers may want to build writers' talk:

1. *Questioning.* If students are sharing their independent work with one another, they can learn to ask appropriate questions to help move their partner forward or help him to take a second look, elaborate, expand, or revise. Possible questions might be:
   - What's the most important part of your piece?
   - Is there more you can tell about that part?
   - This part surprised me . . . can you explain?
   - Are you "showing" or "telling" in this section?
   - What do you plan to do next?

2. *Finding, sharing, and recording information.* As Sharon Roberts showed in the snapshot earlier in the chapter, teachers can assist writers in locating information and resources, discussing their findings, and incorporating the findings into individual or jointly composed pieces. Sharon says, "I really reinforce what resources they have when writing independently . . . we have the word wall . . . all the shared reading texts. They go back and find those words, those concepts. Once we talk about and emphasize that resources are everywhere, they look in their math books for words . . . they revisit old writing pieces, they look around the room for books we've read . . . they check the bulletin board. They find things we've been over eight zillion times, but they also find words like *amphibian* and *reptile* . . . things I don't expect them to spell. They know where to find them!

3. *Making and sharing connections.* Teachers ask students to talk about connections they are making in their individual or co-composed pieces, connections to self, text, and theme (Keene and Zimmerman 1997). Writers also connect to previous writing, reading, and classroom experiences, returning to these resources to reconnect. As Sharon says, "I've seen kids go to partner writing and, through their talk and sharing, they are encouraged to dig back and look for something they've done, because they remember working through it there and now they need it somewhere else . . . for the new piece. So, they go and find it and reapply in a whole new way."

4. *Planning for partner talk.* This can take any form and often changes depending on the genre in which writers research, read, respond, or create original pieces. When asking writers to plan their talk, teachers model, demonstrate, and suggest ways to begin, often providing graphic organizers to help writers collect and organize information. Teachers might ask writing partners to

talk about narrative elements such as plot, setting, and characters; nonfiction text structures and conventions; or surprising, confusing, or favorite parts.

The appendixes offer a variety of graphic organizers.

■ Checking in and Conferring with Writing Partners

While writing partners work, teachers circulate among the groups, checking in, praising, redirecting, noticing instances of supportive interactions, and helping writers to problem solve. If writers are off-task or have misunderstood instructions, the teacher may intervene and redirect; however, if the ultimate goal is writers' independence, teachers are urged not to solve problems for children, but to listen and ask the kinds of questions that will assist writers in helping themselves. Suggestions for checking in include the following:

- Take at least a minute or two to unobtrusively listen from a few feet away.
- Wait for a break in the action before speaking.
- Begin with an open-ended question such as, "how's it going?" before redirecting or clarifying a task.
- Try to ask, not tell, so that writers can confer and solve issues themselves.
- Focus on the writers first, then the writing.
- When suggesting a strategy or idea, ask, "have you tried this?" or say, "you might try this," rather than dictating what they must do.
- Make it clear through your actions, words, and body language that the writers are in charge of their writing.

■ Visual Reminders—Charts and Checklists

In most classrooms where children are paired for writing, teachers work with students to create wall charts or small reminder sheets specifically focused on effective collaboration (Figure 4–1). If we expect writing partners to use these tools, charts and reminder sheets should be created *with students*, not presented to them as a teacher-created framework. This cannot be stressed enough. If students are expected to make use of charts and reminder sheets, teachers should refer to them every time partners write, adding new strategies and ideas to these resources throughout the year.

■ Other Tools for Writing Partners

In addition to reminder sheets and charts, there are other tools teachers can provide writing partners throughout the year. Second-grade teacher Cheryl Feeney provides writers with many tools, some of which are housed in writing buckets (colorful, plastic vertical files) placed on each work table. The contents of Cheryl's writing buckets change throughout the year, but always include:

- children's individual writing folders (blue, red, yellow, green, depending on one's group)
- crayons
- large writing journals
- "seed journals" (these are tiny journals that the children can take home to brainstorm ideas for writing with their parents. Seed journals move from students' homework folders to desks and then to the writing buckets.)
- pens (black and red flair—Cheryl finds these the best writing tools. They are easier to use than pencils—and red is for editing.)
- a box of colored pencils
- Picture dictionaries
- A variety of spelling dictionaries and word books
- "Why I Revise" editing checklist
- Assessing My Revision checklist

FIG. 4–1 *Rules for Writing Partners Chart*

Many of the strategies described in Parts 2 and 3 include tools specific to those models. Like the charts and reminder sheets described here, whenever possible, *tools should be created with writers*, not simply handed to them. Teachers will need to design and choose tools that serve the needs of their students, curriculum, and specific writing tasks. In addition to reference sources such as spelling dictionaries, regular dictionaries, and thesauruses, teachers might consider:

1. *Strategy gloves.* Construct strategy gloves (see Figure 4–2) with each finger outlining a different writing or partner strategy. Ideas for gloves include

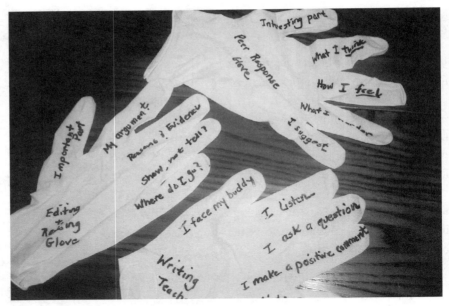

FIG. 4–2 *Strategy Gloves*

white canvas carpentry gloves, rubber gloves, or laminated, paper gloves that children can hold, or that are affixed to tables where writers work.

2. *Strategy bookmarks.* Young readers love bookmarks, especially those they create themselves. In *Snapshots*, Linda Hoyt (2000) suggests making "fix it" bookmarks to remind readers of important strategies. Hoyt also provides blank templates inviting children and teachers to create their own bookmarks (20, 205). Bookmarks that outline important partner strategies and reminders can easily be constructed. Appendix A offers ideas for bookmarks.

Children love to have their personal strategy bookmarks laminated and placed in a Bookmark Can for all to borrow and enjoy. Bookmarks lists might include:

- ways to help my partner
- what to do when writing is hard
- finding resources for writing
- rules for writing partners
- ways to talk about writing with my partner.

3. *Lapdesks.* Lapdesks can be pressed into service to help focus writers' attention while providing a comfortable, contained writing surface. When partners

write, I model the use of a lap desk if I notice they are distracted, with papers flying and pens continually dropping to the floor. I suggest that partners search together for a "just-right pillow," large picture book or folder cardboard "game boards," for this purpose.

4. *"Offices" for writing privacy.* Sometimes the sights and goings on in a busy classroom become too much for writers, distracting them as they try to write. Or writing partners who may be diligently working are subjected to constant interruption or scrutiny from neighboring partnerships. When this happens, I sometimes suggest that writers build themselves an "office" using large, sturdy picture books to create a writing carrel for privacy and focus.

5. *Telephones.* When children read and reread their pieces with partners, voice volume can be a problem. "Reading phones" (see Figure 4–3) made from PVC piping are helpful in minimizing voice volume while maximizing auditory input and encouraging expressive, dramatic reading. These inexpensive elbow pipes can be found in any building supply store.

6. *Genre-specific organizers and genre research sheets.* These tools, familiar supports for individual writers, can also be great vehicles for writing partners' conversation and collaboration. Examples of genre organizers and research sheets are found in Appendix C and discussed in detail in Chapter 14.

7. *Editing and revising checklists.* Important tools to aid writers taking a second look at their pieces, these lists are also helpful when partners act as listeners

and editors for each other. Examples of editing and revising checklists are found in Appendix D and discussed in detail in Chapter 10.

8. *Writing implements.* In many classrooms I visit, teachers have reported dramatic changes in writers' fluency simply by changing from pencils to pens, pens to markers, and so forth. As a writer, this makes perfect sense to me, since I must have a special kind of pen in my hand in order to feel really comfortable writing. Offering students a wide choice of writing implements allows them to find what works best.

9. *Have-a-Go spaces.* Many teachers, like Sharon Roberts, invite writers to make use of "practice spaces" for tentative writing (see Figure 4–3), places to experiment with something before using it in their "real text." Have-a-Go spaces extend from the practice spaces teachers provide for writers during shared and guided writing activities. Such spaces might be found on scrap paper, sticky notes, or along the side, top, or bottom of a writer's paper.

Sharon says, "I give them that Have a Go section to work through something. When we give writers this space, we say, 'it's okay to take a break from that and come over here and work through this thing.' When I do shared or interactive writing, I constantly model this . . . taking a break to work though a tough spot. When we provide this space [children] are much more willing to stop and work through something."

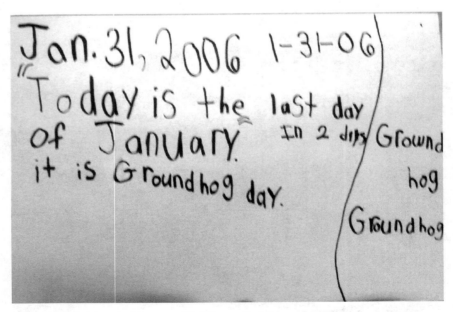

FIG. 4–3 *Community Message with "Have-a-Go" Space*

10. *Paper.* Most writers I know are very particular not only about pens, pencils and markers, but also about the kind of pad, paper, or surface they use for writing. Why should children be any different? Having many types of paper, journals, etc., available to writers makes good sense.

■ Concluding Thoughts

Supporting effective writing partnerships is about listening to what children are telling us they need and what is working. To this end, we want to plan instruction that builds children's skills and strategies, increases their active engagement in all types of composing, and moves them toward confident, independent writing. These goals provide the rationale for including these collaborative contexts in already crowded literacy programs.

5 | Writing Partnerships for English Language Learners

Talk is so beneficial to all my students, especially those learning English . . . and the talk in writing partnerships provides great modeling and practice.

—Second-grade teacher

■ Learning English Through Writing, Talk, and Joint Composing

When children are surrounded by environmental print, shown daily modeling of written language production through shared and interactive writing activities, and introduced to many literary genres through teacher read-alouds, they begin writing very early in their exposure to English (Hudelson 1983). Teachers of young children often watch students literally write their way into reading. Many young children write before they read because writing slows down the reading process and enables them to progress at a comfortable and supportive pace. For students learning English, writing growth may mirror oral language development (Hudelson 1983). "Researchers have found that [a high degree of oral language proficiency is not necessary for children learning English] to successfully communicate their thoughts and experiences in writing" (Samway 2006, 28). Can such writing experiences be further enhanced with a supportive partner by one's side?

The role of talk in developing students' English fluency—both oral and written—has been explored by many researchers (Barnes 1992; Dyson 1983, 1993; Edelsky and Jilbert 1985). In proposing a framework for language acquisition, Cummins (2001) outlines three areas: meaning, language, and use. What English language learners are hearing, reading, and writing must be understandable to them. They must also be aware of semantics, syntax, orthographic cueing systems for reading, and know how to use these language forms to create meaning and interpretively read and reread text. What better way to focus on meaning, language, and use than through conversation with a peer partner? And what more meaningful texts could we give English language learners than those they have created themselves through talking and joint composing?

McCauley and McCauley (1992) identify four important elements for learners acquiring a second language—a low-anxiety environment, repeated practice, comprehensible input, and drama. When undertaken in a caring classroom community, writing partnerships support all four of these elements. All learners need and deserve an environment characterized by trust, respect, and low anxiety. Working with a trusted peer partner on all stages of writing—from prewriting to revision—decreases anxiety and allows English language learners to compose with greater confidence, because they know they can discuss their writing with their buddy.

Writing partnerships provide English language learners with lots of practice as they talk, write, rewrite, and edit. With peers closest to them in development, students learning English have access to the social language most relevant to them in negotiating the complex world of school. When learners use language in social settings, they also make connections between speech and actions (Opitz and Rasinski 1998).

▪ Teacher Roles

Teachers have important roles to play, not only in supporting effective partnerships for English language learners but also in adjusting and modulating instructional approaches to match students' understanding. Teachers of all students, but especially English language learners, should take care to speak clearly and specifically, checking in frequently to make sure students understand. When teaching and modeling effective strategies for writing partnerships, teachers should use multiple ways of presenting material, accompanying oral directions with visual supports whenever possible. Rehearsed, repeated reading activities are tremendously supportive of English language learners. The Authors' Chair provides writers with a forum for dramatic readings of their joint compositions. Before such readings, teachers should encourage writers to practice and rehearse so that readings are fluent, expressive, and successful.

If the goal is to have all students actively involved in writing partnership activities, teachers may want to pay particular attention to ways that their speech, behavior, and instructional approaches reflect "comprehensible input" for children, especially those struggling to learn English (Short 1991). Suggestions for ways to engage all learners are:

1. Pay attention to body language. Use gestures and facial expressions that draw children in and provide a context for your words.
2. Speak clearly and slowly. Practice to be sure you sound natural.
3. Pause frequently between utterances, allowing children to think about and process each segment of instruction.
4. Use vocabulary that is familiar to all students, repeating and reviewing words as much as possible. Allow students to hear and experience familiar vocabulary in different contexts whenever possible.
5. Observe learners carefully for comprehension, restating, reteaching and reclarifying whenever necessary. Use visuals, gestures, and models to support comprehension.
6. Keep discussions open whenever possible, inviting many perspectives and viewpoints.
7. Use visuals and graphic organizers and model how to use them for writing in many contexts.
8. Communicate through many modalities—oral, written, physical, and pictorial.
9. Provide hands-on practice and collaborative exploration.
10. Model what you expect from writers frequently, being careful to provide instruction for different learning styles and preferences.
11. Vary writing approaches to respond to all learning styles and preferences.

■ Children's Literature as a Catalyst for Writing

Using literature models or mentor texts supports all learners, but may be particularly helpful for English language learners. Texts with familiar real-life situations, themes, structures, and patterns are particularly useful for English language learners. For example, using a book like Charlotte Zolotow's (1965)

Someday with its imaginative story and refrain of "someday" provides a supportive structure that writers can mimic in writing their own "someday stories." For more about using literature models see Chapters 14 and 18.

When choosing literature models to share with students learning English, Lado (2006) recommends beginning with here-and-now topics, which are transparent and easy to understand. I also recommend beginning with shorter texts with limited complexity of subject matter and grammar. Such texts should be read and reread slowly with expression, taking care to pause frequently for questions and discussion of vocabulary and concepts. Once students are comfortable with the structure and have gained some fluency reading these texts, they can take the next step to use them as models for their independent or partner writing. A helpful sequence when using texts as models for English language learners' writing would be:

The teacher
1. Introduces a text, discussing key vocabulary and concepts before reading.
2. Reads text slowly and dramatically.
3. Rereads several times, pausing to discuss content, vocabulary, and structure.

The students
4. Reread the text with their partner.
5. Examine the text with their partner, paying particular attention to structure, plot, characters or whatever elements the teacher has identified as a focus.
6. Share their findings with the whole class.

These experiences give students valuable practice with continuous written English. Writers also learn new vocabulary and concepts and make important discoveries about written English that they can use when they write alone or with partners. Such activities may lead directly to partner writing, where students co-compose original texts modeled after the mentor text.

If a student is able to read in her first language, quality literature written in that language could act as a powerful model for writing and allow the writer to share her language and culture with peers. (See the resource list at the end of this chapter, in particular the Culture for Kids website.)

■ Writing Strategies for English Language Learners

Each chapter in Parts 2 and 3 describes a partnership model teachers can easily incorporate into their existing writing programs. At the conclusion of each chapter, suggestions are given for using, adapting, or extending the strategy for

English language learners. Like all learners, students working to master English respond and grow when teachers use research-based, best literacy practices. That said, English language learners frequently find themselves surrounded by native speakers with levels of receptive and expressive English vocabularies far exceeding their own. In responding to the needs of these children, teachers may want to incorporate some of the following practices and approaches, which are particularly supportive of English language learners. Teachers are encouraged to seek out additional ways as well to help English language learners plunge into writing and other literate activities as full participants.

Language Experience

The language approach began as a strategy for English language learners and has a long history of use with students mastering English (Nelson and Linek 1999). The approach has much support as an effective early literacy strategy, particularly for second language learners (Garcia 1974). Like shared and guided writing activities, language experience involves lots of discussion characterized by a high degree of student and teacher use of language. The teacher then writes down what children say, modeling how oral language is encoded into print. Children observe this process, are asked to read and reread the created text, and are often given follow-up activities for use with this jointly constructed text.

Language experience activities integrate all literate processes of reading, writing, listening, and speaking. They also:

- promote greater involvement of individual students
- motivate all learners, inviting them into literate activities
- value student backgrounds, cultures, and experiences as students' words and thoughts become "the text"
- enable all students to participate at their own level on a continuum of language skills (Nelson and Linek 1999)
- value and celebrate all perspectives.

Procedures for Language Experience   There are many variations on this approach, some of which are described in subsequent chapters. The basic steps are as follows:

1. The teacher *initiates a class discussion* about a familiar subject, topic, or experience. Topics might be a classroom pet, a field trip, a familiar story retold, or an original story using a familiar structure (e.g., writing a variation of a Cinderella tale after hearing and discussing many other versions). The choice of topics is endless and depends on the interests of the teacher and students.
2. After much discussion, the teacher *asks for students' contributions.*
3. Ideally, *every child contributes* at least one sentence to a language experience text. The teacher writes students' words verbatim on a chart or whiteboard large enough for all to see.
4. Throughout the composing process, *the teacher invites students to assist in reading* and rereading text.
5. *Students are later given individual copies of the text* created to reread and, perhaps, illustrate.
6. Once completed, *individual stories are sent home* for students to keep and reread for practice.

Follow-up activities such as word work and writing responses might also be used depending on the needs of students and program. For teachers who want to learn more, an excellent resource for using the language experience approach is Nelson and Linek's book (1999) *Practical Classroom Applications of Language Experience: Looking Back, Looking Forward.*

Connecting Language Experience and Writing Partnerships   This strategy provides powerful modeling of the writing process for English language learners. As a prewriting activity, teachers make explicit connections between their modeling of process and the co-composing work partners will subsequently be expected to undertake. One possible sequence for all writers, especially those learning English would be:

1. The teacher and students discuss and jointly compose a language experience story with the teacher acting as scribe.
2. Partners read, reread, and illustrate individual copies of the story, coming together to share observations and work with the whole class.
3. The teacher introduces a particular writing model where partners are expected to co-compose a text using the structure and model of the previous language experience story.
4. The teacher gives explicit instructions to partners about how to proceed.
5. Partners co-compose, either sharing the pen or with one partner acting as scribe.
6. Partners share their piece with the whole class.

Thematic Learning Approaches

Thematic learning approaches support all learners, especially those learning English. Using a theme provides a focus for teachers and students around which new and acquired vocabulary can be used again and again in different contexts. When involved in thematic units of study, teachers should pay particular attention to vocabulary for their English language learners because these children "cannot express in English everything they think" (Nelson and Linek 1999, 240) and must be supported in incorporating new vocabulary and concepts into their receptive and expressive repertoire.

A theme might not necessarily be a topic. Thematic learning approaches entail exploration and extending students' thinking to "find issues, make inquiries, and arrive at judgments" (Sebesta 1994, 2). Since this kind of active exploration and inquiry is challenging for English language learners, the support of a partner often ensures greater success and feelings of confidence and competence.

Planning Considerations for Thematic Study   "It is possible for ESL teachers to select themes based on the magnitude of vocabularies found in academic concepts" (Nelson and Linek, 1999, 241). Nelson and Linek suggest that while units on such topics as dinosaurs or teddy bears may be charming, they may not be as useful or supportive in developing vocabulary of English language learners as units on clothing, food, or occupations. Therefore, in choosing topics for thematic units, teachers are encouraged to select wisely, with an eye to facilitating *all* children's language and vocabulary development.

Connecting Thematic Learning Approaches and Writing Partnerships There are many ways teachers can effectively incorporate English language learners into thematic study partnerships. Many of the models described in Parts 2 and 3 relate to thematic units of study and suggest ways partner writing and research can be integrated. Some of these are as follows:

- Partners ask "big questions" about a topic, then share.
- Partners gather and explore resources on the topic or question.
- Partners take notes, complete graphic organizers, and plan writing pieces together.
- Partners co-compose text related to thematic study.
- Partners edit and revise together.

Drawing, Talking, and Writing Approaches

English language learners sometimes struggle to express ideas in writing or speaking. Taylor (1990) found that newly arrived immigrant students used symbols and pictures to express ideas "because of the thrifty way they convey embedded meaning" (111). Inviting English language learners to use symbols, pictures, and other visuals in their writing supports their nascent attempts to express their thinking. Modeling and sharing rebus stories is one fun way to introduce symbol use for writers. Another strategy specifically designed to encourage English language learners' use of symbols and pictures is described here, but teachers can encourage writers to use pictures to express thoughts, ideas and information.

"Read–Talk–Draw–Write" Lado's (2006) Read–Talk–Draw–Write strategy incorporates all literate processes as children work together to create text. Similar to retelling and rewriting, this strategy helps children extract and use information in stories they hear and read. The procedure is as follows:

1. The teacher chooses a short text selection.
2. The teacher introduces relevant vocabulary—including names, actions, labels, captions, etc.—before reading a story.
3. The teacher reads and rereads dramatically.

4. The teacher teaches English in the text through a series of guiding questions.
5. The students choose and draw something from the text illustrating new vocabulary.
6. The students copy names, labels, and captions from text.
7. The text is bound or published on the wall of the classroom.

Drawing and Writing in Partnerships   This strategy works well with individual writers as well as with partnerships. When writers work together, they may co-compose writing and illustrations or divide tasks in ways that suit them. Teachers may provide structures and guidelines, such as "everybody writes, everybody draws," or let partners decide. Whatever way teachers choose to incorporate a drawing–writing strategy, they may want to allow and encourage English language learners to use visuals and pictures anytime they are useful in supporting writing fluency and expression.

Genre Studies

If writing is not a linear process of acquiring skills in a set sequence, but rather a recursive endeavor where learners are continually reorganizing, regressing, and jumping forward (Edelsky and Jilbert 1985), then a deliberate focus on the structure, conventions and style of specific genres (such as poetry, realistic fiction, mystery, biography, and many others) supports all learners' development, particularly those learning English.

This strategy for writing buddies is described in detail in Chapter 14. However, in order to provide as many contextual experiences for English language learners as possible, teachers may want to embed genre studies into all aspects of their curriculum.

Suggestions for Genre Studies with English Language Learners   If we expect partners or individuals to write in a particular genre, we must provide explicit instruction and modeling and give students repeated exposure to literary examples of the genre through reading aloud. During a deliberate study of a genre, such as nonfiction, teachers and students would read and examine a text, discussing its structure, conventions, and content. Talk might center around text structures such as cause and effect, chronology, comparison and contrast, or problem and solution. Discussion of the qualities found in a persuasive text or a rich, descriptive narrative also serves to focus writers' attention on genre.

When exploring genre with learners who are then expected to produce genre specific writing pieces, teachers may want to follow this sequence:

1. The teacher reads and shares many examples of the genre.
2. The teacher reads and shares her own genre-specific writing.
3. The teacher dissects, examines, and discusses with students genre structures and conventions.
4. The teacher creates a chart, outline, map, or diagram with students illustrating clearly the writing criteria for a particular genre.
5. The teacher invites writers to plan and write their own genre-specific pieces.
6. The students write genre pieces individually or in partnerships, using structures and criteria provided.
7. The students edit and revise writing pieces for publications.
8. The students share with the whole class.

This sequence can be used with all learners. In order to ensure English language learners' success with genre writing, teachers might want to provide additional small-group or individual genre exploration times where literature models or mentor texts are reread and examined and vocabulary and concepts are reinforced, clarified, and applied in many contexts.

■ Concluding Thoughts

Through discussion and joint composing, writers learning English build background knowledge that allows them to more fully participate in all literate pursuits. Whether writing to one another in dialogue journals, a frequently used strategy for English language learners (Johnson and Roen 1989; Hudelson 1989; Peyton 1990; Peyton and Reed 1990), or researching and discussing a mutually interesting topic, working with a partner supports all children's writing development. Opportunities to compose, preread, and practice text and discuss concepts and ideas builds English language learners' background about subject matter, syntax, and vocabulary. Experiencing words, phrases, and language structures in a variety of writing context strengthens reading comprehension of English language learners.

■ Resources

Useful websites for supporting English language learners:

www.everythingesl.net: Teaching suggestions and lesson plans for using literature with English language learners.

www.realbooks.co.uk: Lists of good books for students learning English.

www.cultureforkids.com: This company sells bilingual books in many languages, a very helpful resource for writers!

Two resources with book lists of literature supportive of English language learners:

HADAWAY, N., S. VERDELL, AND T. YOUNG. 2002. *Literature-Based Instruction with English Language Learners*. Boston: Allyn & Bacon.

SPRANGENBERG-URBSCHAT, K., AND R. PRITCHARD. 1994. *Kids Come in All Languages: Reading Instruction for ESL Students*. Newark, DE: International Reading Association.

Adapting the Model: Using Writing Partnerships with All Learners

6

I like working with a partner because you don't have to study on your own. [The writing partner] makes me feel more confident because, it's like, I'm not working with someone who goes, "Oh, you spelled that word wrong." It's like, "I know that! I can do that!" when I'm with my partner.

—Fifth-grade special needs student

CLASSROOM CHALLENGE

How do I meet the writing needs of all learners, especially my special needs students?

■ Adapting the Model for All Learners: What Does It Entail?

"Students who have a long history of difficulty with language need to be active participants in social activities that include conversation" (Nelson and Linek 1999, 232). Conversation and dialogue, help all students work beyond their mastery level as long as activities are still within their problem-solving capability. With the right context and support, all learners can productively share ideas and expertise with one another. Because each learner's zone of proximal development (Vygotsky 1978) is different, teachers get to know each individual student through observation, assessment, and daily interactions so that appropriate learning experiences can be planned. In differentiating instruction, teachers may also want to accept a range of written responses depending upon the skills and developmental level of learners.

The strategies and writing partnership models described thus far can be tweaked, adapted, and tailored to suit all learners. Social support for writing should, and easily can be, available to every student regardless of ability and developmental level. This chapter does not necessarily present new material; rather, it discusses how to use what we already have with all students.

■ Christine's Writers

Christine Mikalyzk's fifth-grade writing partners are co-composing biographies of famous people. They have collaborated through every stage of the writing process—from selection of a subject to research, reading, note taking, and outlining. The day that I observe, they are co-composing the first drafts of their biographies, with each partnership deciding how this writing will happen. Some partnerships alternate scribing duties every few sentences or every paragraph; others have worked out structures that work for them while adhering to Christina's requirement that both partners share the writing.

I check in with Roger and Melony, who are collaborating on a biography of Ronald Reagan. They are seated catty-corner to each other, working on their first draft; their notes and outlines are scattered around them. First, they discuss what they will write, then, as Roger writes down their thoughts, Melony types the same text on her "Alpha-smart" computer. They check each other's paper frequently and make adjustments and revisions as needed. When their first draft is complete, they will choose which copy—Roger's handwritten one or Melony's typed version—to edit and revise for their final copy.

Christina tells me later that Melony's development level is several grades below most of the fifth graders, but she has "really risen to the occasion" on the biography project and has been very involved. Christine also tells me, "This project, with all its steps and procedures, particularly using outlines and researching in all kinds of sources, is new for many of my students, but something I know they will be doing next year [in middle school]. I thought, for the first exposure, working with a partner would help them see how it's done and be able to discuss each segment so they won't be totally overwhelmed next year when they're asked to do these things alone."

When I interview Melony, she echoes Christine's words, emphasizing that working with a partner, "makes me feel more comfortable and really want to do something well." Melony also enjoys, "having a friend . . . I get to make a new friend."

■ Writing Partnerships for All Learners

When I interviewed Melony, in addition to telling me how much she enjoyed working with her current partner, Roger, she also told me about previous experiences that did not work so well.

> Last year, I was working with a partner, a person I was doing it [writing] with, and it was like . . . he had to do everything. And, everything you [I] said was wrong. So it was like, "alright, I don't want to do it your way, why don't we try it a new way?" And, he was like, "no, I don't want to do it that way," and I was like . . . oh, please, just stop, just do it and leave me alone. That was hard. He's [Roger, her fifth-grade partner] not like that.

Roger is, indeed, a patient, supportive partner to Melony, but what Melony does not acknowledge are the instruction and frameworks her teacher, Ms. Mikalyzk, has provided for them. As with all writing partnerships, successful, effective collaboration does not "just happen," but needs the support and guidance of teacher modeling, specific minilessons, and clear expectations. This takes into account many dimensions of a particular learning task such as the needs of each individual writer, the social dynamics of each partnership, considerations about content (e.g., do students have background and familiarity with content?), the availability and accessibility of appropriate resources, and task requirements and expectations.

According to Nelson and Linek (1999), teachers also plan minilessons for students that:

- Frame their thoughts and words.
- Listen to the meaning of their message.
- Help them to structure and clarify.
- Help them to expand vocabulary choices, correct inaccuracies or confusions.
- Help them elaborate on the content of their message.
- Provide tools and resources to help with all stages of writing, from planning to organization, composing, editing, and revision.

These goals can be realized through a gradual release of responsibility for writing tasks to children where

1. Careful modeling of the process *precedes partners' work.*
2. Teachers carefully select appropriate writing partnership strategies and models, then adapt them to suit all learners.
3. Teachers pair children in ways that serve their individual learning strengths and needs.
4. Teachers provide the tools and resources each learner needs to be successful.

Modeling and Shared Text

Daily creation of shared text—teacher and students—models not only process but also the active participation of all learners. During a whole-class shared or guided writing activity, the four steps listed are addressed—through conversation, reading, and rereading; teacher and student questioning; and specific, focused teaching. If we want all learners to experience success in partnerships and independent writing, we must provide daily experiences for creation of the kind of shared text—genre, style, and form—that we expect writers to produce. A sequence for such work might look like this:

1. *Introduce a new genre, style, or writing form through many read-aloud sessions.* These read-aloud sessions should provide time to pause, examine, and talk about the text in question.

2. *Discuss and dissect the teacher's written model of the genre, style, or form.* The teacher follows the read-aloud session by modeling an example of the genre, style, or form. Typically, students of all ages love to critique their teacher's written work. Discussing and dissecting another's writing elicits important vocabulary and concepts about form and content. From such discussions, students might produce charts and outlines that can then be posted on classroom walls to act as resources for writers. Teachers can make effective use of student writing from previous classes—anonymous, of course—in this same way. When chosen carefully, student writing often provides more effective, developmentally appropriate models for children than does adult writing.

3. *Write shared text daily.* Using the criteria and expertise derived from the earlier activities, everyone participates in creating *several examples* of shared text in a particular genre, style, or form.

4. *Small groups create shared text.* If some students need further modeling, teaching, or conversation before working in partnership, the teacher can pull a small group together while others begin partner work.

5. *Partners create text.* By the time partners reach this phase of a unit of study, they have language, tools, resources, and understandings to bring to the creation of their paired text.

Writing Partnership Models and Adaptations to Suit All Learners

As Roger and Melony show us, all students can be research buddies if roles are clearly defined and modified. Teachers are encouraged to try any model or strategy described throughout the book, providing appropriate modification for their students. Here I introduce a few writing partnership models and suggestions for working with students of differing abilities. Teachers will, no doubt, have many more ideas that suit individuals in their classrooms.

Echo Writing Echo writing is a natural for writers of differing abilities. One writer writes while the other copies or echoes. If this is used as a warm-up for writing, I recommend that teachers suspend requirements for spelling and mechanics and allow both partners the chance to be the writer and echoer, each writing one to two sentences, then stopping to discuss. Another variation I've used is to have the less-experienced writer act as "teller" and the stronger writer act as scribe, then both discuss.

Dialogue Journals   When guidelines are clear and the emphasis is on communication and meaning, not mechanics, dialogue journals—written conversations between learners—can be wonderful partner-writing vehicles. Partners should understand that their role is to communicate their thoughts and to hear and respond to the thoughts of their partner, not act as an editor or the "spelling police." When ability levels differ widely, it is important to emphasize the importance of:

- Reading for meaning and understanding
- Asking for clarification through respectful questioning.

Writer/Illustrator   One writer writes, the other illustrates. In this case, both would decide on, or compose, what is to be said and illustrated before writers begin.

Joint Composing   Whether partners are writing fiction, nonfiction, or poetry together, when ability levels differ widely, one way to support all learners' participation is to be a bit more creative in dividing writing tasks. In the snapshot earlier, Christine Mikalyzk modifies writing work so that Melony can fully participate while receiving writing support from her partner, Roger—a much stronger writer. Both writers talk and discuss ideas, and decide what they want to say. As each writes what they have decided on, Roger's handwritten model serves as a resource for Melony when she is unsure of how to spell or write a word. *Both writers are composing* in this scenario, which, after all, is the ultimate goal of any writing project.

I believe tactile involvement is very supportive of all learners; therefore, whenever possible, I encourage teachers to define structures where both writers hold the pen. Sometimes, depending on students' learning needs, joint composing might involve only one partner acting as scribe. Both partners create or "write" the text through discussion and decision making about what they want to say, but only one acts as scribe. In Roger and Melony's case, the more capable writer holds the pen, but I have also seen partnerships where a less-experienced writer scribes while her more capable peer dictates word by word, or even letter by letter, how text should be written.

Pairing Decisions for All Learners

In most instances, I recommend forming partnerships where readers and writers work with peers closest to their ability and developmental level; however, when making decisions to support all learners' participation, teachers may need to make creative decisions about pairing. The following partners may better support the needs of special learners:

- *Adult.* A child with special needs is paired with a classroom aide, adult volunteer, or the teacher for partner-writing activities.
- *Older student.* Many schools require middle and high school–age students to complete community service or service learning projects each year or prior to graduation. These older, more experienced writers can be trained to be wonderful, supportive partners for special needs students.
- *More capable peer.* Careful pairing of children within a classroom—like Roger and Melony's fifth-grade partnership—can allow all writers to more fully participate in a task, project, or activity that would be too difficult for them alone. As with all partnerships, teachers must provide *both partners* with appropriate modeling, training, and clear expectations for how these partnerships will work.

Tools for All Learners

All writing buddies benefit from visual reminders, graphic organizers, reference tools (word walls, word books, dictionaries, thesauruses, etc.), editing checklists, and classroom charts. Special needs learners do not necessarily need additional tools, but may need individual copies of resource materials, wall charts, and visuals so that these resources are at their fingertips rather than hanging on a wall across the classroom. Teachers or classroom volunteers can transcribe wall charts and group-created visuals, providing partners with individual copies. Tools, charts, checklists, and other resources can also be augmented with additional cues in the form of illustrations and pictures to aid all learners.

7

Home Connections: Writing Partnerships Outside of School

When I do a [writing] project, I usually have my grandpa draw a picture for me and . . . uh, I tape it to the piece of paper and I read it with my partner. My grandpa is an expert artist.

—Fifth grader

CLASSROOM CHALLENGE

How can I find more time to give students the writing practice and support they need?

■ Why Take Writing Partnerships Home?

Encouraging family members and caregivers to complete fun, collaborative writing projects at home gives all learners extra time and support to strengthen skills, strategies, and confidence as composers. Most parents and caregivers want to help their children, but they may not know how. School expectations may not be clear or parents may lack confidence in their own writing skills. Adults or older siblings may also be too busy with housework or their own work and the thought of taking on yet another project seems overwhelming. Also, students may balk at working with loved ones because they do not want to risk failing with those they hold most dear. One of my own sons loved reading and writing with me, the other did not. We take our cues from children.

Whether we are working with students for whom English is a first or second language, making home–school connections is a powerful means of supporting young writers. Keeping certain guidelines in mind, teachers and schools can tap into the rich "fund of knowledge" or "cultural resources" within each home and community that are often neglected in "doing the curriculum" (Moll and Diaz 1993).

When sending writing activities home, teachers should:

- Choose comfortable, low-risk activities.
- Make sure that students clearly understand expectations, structures, and guidelines.
- Choose fun, engaging activities.
- Choose activities connected in some way to life at home whenever possible.
- Emphasize content over mechanics.
- Give clear guidelines about expectations in relation to mechanics— grammar, spelling, and proofreading.
- Choose activities that allow children to share their culture, heritage, and interests.
- Choose activities that encourage the use of more than one linguistic system.
- Choose activities that make use of home resources.

■ Ideas and Strategies for Home-Based Writing Partnerships

The possibilities for home-based writing partnerships are limitless and depend on needs of students, classroom and curriculum. The following ideas are merely suggestions meant to jump-start teachers' thinking about the possibilities for taking writing partnerships home. Many of the strategies described in Parts 2 and 3 of this book make great home writing-partnership activities and are included here with suggestions for adapting for home writing buddies. Activities teachers send home should be fun, relevant, authentic, and not too time-consuming.

1. *Literature response journals and "book bags."* Many primary classrooms send book bags home with a read-aloud book and related activities for parents and children to enjoy. Including a co-composing activity for children and parents in book bags makes supportive connections to reading responses students are expected to do at school.

2. *Echo writing.* This is a perfect adult–child writing activity that is low risk and easy for parents and children to adapt in a variety of ways. Outlined in Chapter 8, echo writing involves first one writer who scribes, followed by her partner, who copies exactly what she has written. Then they switch. When sending echo writing home as a partner-writing activity, teachers will want to:

   - Specify length and expectations for mechanic errors.
   - Provide guidelines that allow both adult and child to be the leader and echoer.
   - Make the writing relevant to the home setting.
   - Keep length short (no more than a paragraph, or two at most).
   - Provide ideas for echo writing topics, such as:
     - observations around the house or neighborhood
     - descriptions of family
     - descriptions of a favorite activity
     - a favorite family meal or recipe.

3. *Dialogue journals.* Once students are familiar with dialogue journals, they can take this strategy home using their classroom journal or a special home dialogue journal. Teachers may want to read or review Chapter 9 to familiarize themselves with this writing-partner strategy. In addition, when using home dialogue journals, teachers may want to:

   - Provide specific prompts for journal entries in the beginning, then vary expectations, sometimes assigning topics and other times allowing free dialogue.
   - Outline specific expectations for length and mechanics.
   - Use sparingly to preserve the fun and spontaneity of this reflective kind of writing.

4. *Buddy biographies.* What better way to share family heritage than by asking adults and children to write "buddy biographies" of each other or other family members? Length and expectations vary according to the age and grade level of writers, but encouraging writers to use illustrations and other visuals is highly recommended.

5. *Joint story writing.* Providing specific guidelines for story writing, such as the narrative charts and maps in Appendix J, can be a wonderful way to get children's story writing jump-started at home. Adults or older siblings can act as buddies to assist younger writers in completing a planning tool such as a story map. Students then bring these to school, ready to draft their stories. Children could also bring home completed graphic organizers and write a first draft with their home writing buddies. There are many

variations, including those where children and adult partners write complete stories together.

6. *Resource buddies.* Parents or caregivers can be enlisted to help their children gather resource materials—books, magazines, newspapers, Web research—that are then brought to school for a writing project. Research materials can also be sent home with instructions for home buddies to read and help students take notes that are then used during school-based writing projects.

7. *Scribe and illustrator.* Just as the name implies, one partner scribes, the other illustrates. This is fun for students of all ages, but especially primary-grade writers. Adult scribes provide powerful models for young writers and allow them to enjoy the process from a low-risk vantage point. Most often, adults take the scribing role and children illustrate, but the roles of scribe and illustrator can shift. As always, teachers should make role expectations clear when sending information home.

8. *Comprehension skills in our world.* A favorite activity of mine, this is really many activities, and is limited only by the number of comprehension and thinking strategies teachers can generate. Basically, home-based writing partners are asked to observe something—an event, television show, or movie—then discuss or write about a specific comprehension skill. In general, it is recommended that *writing be brief* and discussion expansive. For example, when watching any event, television show, or movie, partners could:
   - Find the main idea.
   - Make a prediction (something to do during commercials!).
   - Draw a conclusion at the conclusion of a television story or program (what would logically happen next?).
   - Write a summary (a few sentences or quick sketches).
   - Bring writing to school to share.

9. *Collecting "home vocabulary."* Home-based writing partners collect and list vocabulary and words used around their home. The possibilities for this activity are infinite, but teachers may want to specify certain kinds of words for partners to search and collect; for example, vocabulary or words from items visible when you walk into the kitchen. Vocabulary associated with a specific person. Children typically love this activity, and their lists are often colorful and varied. We may want to specify "no profanity," but usually home writing buddies figure this out without guidance.

10. *Collecting particular kinds of words.* Writers of all ages love to collect words, particularly if there is a vehicle for sharing them at school. I

have asked kindergartners and fifth graders to search for certain kinds of words *we were studying in our curriculum,* which I then add to charts and wall displays around the classroom (see Figure 7–1). One morning, a first grader presented me with seventy-four homophones she had brainstormed with her writing buddy—her dad. Children of all ages seem to delight in enlisting home partners to generate lists of particular kinds of words, such as:

- compound words
- homographs (words that are spelled the same, but have different meanings and, sometimes, pronunciation—such as "sow," to scatter, and "sow," a female pig)
- homophones (words that sound the same, but are spelled differently and have different meanings, such as "knight" and "night")
- synonyms
- antonyms
- words that begin with a particular letter
- words with silent e
- words with consonant clusters
- words with a particular "rime" (-at, -ip, etc.)
- multisyllable words (two-syllable, three-syllable, etc.)
- contractions

FIG. 7–1 *Homonym "Pear/Pair" Tree*

■ Other Considerations

In addition to including clear instructions when sending home a writing activity or project, it is important to always provide a vehicle for parents and students to respond, give feedback, and ask questions. This might be a journal response sheet or even a checklist with space for comments. Unless response forms are very simple, I give students and parents the option of whether to respond. This might not work for some teachers, who may require this step as a means to ascertain whether an activity was used and how it went. Response and feedback may be desirable, regularly or occasionally, depending on the type of writing we are asking students and caregivers to engage in.

Whether or not children have been regularly read to or involved in reading and writing activities at home, they all come to school with literacies that we want to embrace and celebrate. Home-based partnerships are the perfect way to do that. As Allen, a first grader, says in telling me about his home-based buddy, "It's a great friend to have a [writing] buddy. I think everyone in the world should have one. He [my grandfather] talks with me and I love him very much."

8 Echo Writing

I'm not lonely.

—Third-grade boy's response when asked what he liked
about writing with a partner

■ Echo Writing: What Is It?

Echo writing jump-starts the writing process, and provides a fun, warm-up activity for writers of all ages. In echo writing, just as the name implies, one partner writes, then the other echoes, writing exactly what the first has written. Then they switch roles. Most teachers specify that the switch take place sentence by sentence. With younger writers you might switch word by word or every couple of words. With older writers, the switch may occur paragraph by paragraph.

Generally, partners echo write for ten to twenty minutes. This strategy is an exercise, like quickwrites (Routman 2000), and as such should not be overused. Echo writing could be used once or twice a week, or less frequently, providing a means for teachers to help students flex their writing muscles. Once children are comfortable working together, sharing ideas and writing strategies, they can move on to other types of writing. Typically, writers of all ages enjoy echoing each other to build a story, poem, or nonfiction writing piece together.

■ The Strategy in Action

Jenny and Marco sit side by side, leaning against cushions in the classroom library area, clipboards on their knees, pencils poised. They are writing a short descriptive piece about yesterday's field trip to the New England Aquarium in Boston. So far, their story reads:

> We rode on the bus to Bostin. Our techers, Ms. Bianco and Mrs. Felix sat in the back. The moms that cam wer Taylor's, Jenny's, Patrick's and Rob's. Greg's dad cam too.

The writers have the same story written on their paper.

Jenny: Okay, your turn.

Marco: We brought . . . no, we took . . . no, we had clipboards for the scavenger hunt. Yup, that's the next one.

Jenny: Okay, write!

Marco: (*writes on his paper*) We ~~brk~~ had clipbords to the . . .

Jenny: No, it should be "for"

Marco: Yup. (*crosses out* to the *and writes*) *for the skavengr hunt.*

Jenny: (*copies this sentence onto her paper*) *We had clipbords for the scavenger hunt.*

Marco: (*studies Jenny's sentence, then changes the spelling of* scavenger *on his paper*) Okay, your turn.

Jenny: Okay, mine [her sentence] will be . . . The first thing we saw was the seals. (*writes*) *The frst thing we saw was the seels.*

Marco: (*points to* frst *on Jenny's paper*)

Jenny: Oops! (*adds* an i *to* first *to spell the word correctly*)

Marco: (*copies Jenny's sentence exactly as she has written it*)

These second graders are engaged in echo writing, a simple, enjoyable way for partners to get comfortable working together. This is their third experience with this type of writing and soon their teacher will transition them to dialogue journals (see Chapter 9). Right now she is using echo writing as a fun way to introduce writing partnerships in her classroom.

■ Steps and Procedures for Echo Writing

As with all the models presented in this book, teachers are encouraged to adapt and change the procedures to serve the needs of their students and program. Basic guidelines are given here, but steps and directions will vary considerably depending on the genre, content, and task in which writers are engaged.

Basic Guidelines for Echo Writing

1. Writers decide who will start as "writing leader" and "echoer."
2. The leader writes a specified segment of text (a word, phrase, sentence, paragraph, etc.).
3. The echoer observes the writing, then copies, or echoes, exactly what the leader has written.
4. Then writers switch roles and—the echoer becomes the leader, and so forth.
5. The pattern repeats.

When in the "echoing" role, writers may or may not offer suggestions about spelling, mechanics, grammar, and content. Unless I observe this kind of assistance becoming problematic—with one writer highly critical of the other—I usually allow children to work this out themselves. In the snapshot, Marco, an English language learner, uses an awkward preposition, "to," instead of "for" and Jenny corrects him. He accepts her suggestion good-naturedly and makes the correction. The teacher could have noted this exchange and raised the issue of supportive assistance as part of a minilesson during the next partner-writing time. The best way I know to encourage students' supportive assistance is to ask their peers to model their behaviors. I might also ask the whole group, "what do you do when you see something in your partner's writing that needs fixing up? Can you show me?" Children learn a lot from this kind of demonstration, much more than they would if I demonstrated or simply told them my expectations.

■ Minilessons and Ideas to Support Echo Writing

Depending on the content, the genre of writing, and the writers themselves, echo writing can take many forms. Minilessons introduce students to echo writing variations; the possibilities are endless. Teachers should choose ideas that serve their students and program. Here are few ideas to get started:

- writing poems and songs together, line by line
- writing silly stories to practice rhyming
- writing patterned or structured stories and poems (For more on structured writing, see Chapter 12.)
  - Begin each line with a repeated phrase such as "I like . . . , I can . . . , I imagine . . ."
  - Use a concept to begin and end a poem, such as "night" (see Figure 8–1).

- Writing chants to practice facts and information across the curriculum
- Creating word lists in alphabetical order
- Writing "telephone stories"
  1. The leader whispers what he will write.
  2. The leader writes out of view of the echoer.
  3. The echoer writes what she has heard.
  4. Partners show each other their writing.
- Writing "people poems" (see Appendix G) (Note: in this variation of echo writing, partners produce different text depending on their interests and personal information, but they collaborate line-by-line about expectations.)
  1. The leader writes the first line.
  2. The echoer writes the first line, substituting her information (name, etc.).
  3. Partners switch.
- Cross-age echo writing (either buddy can begin; the leader and echoer switch as in other models)

FIG. 8–1 *"Night" Poem*

Teachers and students will find their own unique ways to incorporate echo writing into literacy programs. It is a quick, simple activity that lends itself to practicing skills and introducing new concepts. It is also a fun way to begin writing partnerships. Echo writing is an ideal, independent writing activity for a buddy writing center. Once routines are established, all that would change is the genre of writing or particular task or content focus.

■ Moving Toward Independence

Echo writing requires at least two writers so by definition it is always a collaborative activity. Children can be encouraged to take the strategy home and try with parents, siblings, or caregivers, then bring their echo-writing pieces to school to share.

■ Suggestions for English Language Learners

Echo writing in all its variations is very supportive of students learning English. A variation of echo writing that provides a bit more structure is what Nelson and Linek (1999) call Expectation Sentences (244). In Expectation Sentences, teachers provide a structure for partners and writers to follow the echo-writing sequence using this structure. See Appendix G for an Expectation Sentences form to use with writing buddies.

Dialogue Journals 9

You do a little bit of work and a little bit of playing and stuff. We laugh a lot. It's fun . . . to like . . . play with them and also do our work.

—Second grader's thoughts about partner writing

■ Dialogue Journals: What Are They?

This strategy invites writers to begin written conversations with each other through dialogue journaling with the emphasis on *communication, not mechanics.* Dialogue journals (Atwell 1987; Daniels and Bizar 1998; Harwayne 2001; Staton 1980, 1987; Wollman-Bonilla 1989) are a form of reflective writing used in many ways in many settings. The benefits of such writing are well documented (Atwell 1985; D'Arcy 1987; Graves 1983; Hall and Robinson 1994; Kooy and Wells 1996). Dialogue journaling can be initiated between teacher and student or between students. While the teacher-to-student journals are supportive of any age writer, the variation of dialogue journaling outlined below is student to student, where children converse with writing partners.

■ Strategy in Action

First graders Pete and Freddie sit on opposite ends of a long, classroom work table. Pete is reading a joke and riddle book while Freddie writes in a spiral-bound notebook with a thin, black marker. A few minutes later, Freddie stops, caps his pen and calls, "okay!" to Pete. He then leans over, grabbing a large toy dump truck parked beside his chair, places it on the table, points it toward Pete and calls, "Here it comes." He places the journal and marker in the truck bed and sends it rolling down the table toward Pete.

Laughing, Pete catches the truck, retrieves the journal and pen, places the joke and riddle book into the truck, and sends it back to Freddie. Pete opens the journal, takes up the marker, and begins writing. As he writes, Freddie flips through the book, occasionally peeking up to check his partner's progress.

These children are engaged in a spirited session of dialogue journaling during a "freewrite" writers workshop. It is late November and they are already accustomed to dialogue journaling with me. Only recently, I have invited them to dialogue with their writing buddies. Freddie and Pete decide on the truck delivery system and also choose where they will write and what they will write about. As it happens on this particular day, they are sharing jokes and riddles with each other. When they inform me of their intention during whole-class sharing, my only requirement is that they not copy directly from the book, hence the shuttling back and forth of the joke and riddle book *away from the writer*. When I read their entries later, I find they have used ideas from the book, but have also used "creative tinkering" to alter the jokes and riddles, making them uniquely their own.

Since this was a "freewrite day," Freddie and Pete have chosen to share jokes and riddles in their dialogue journals. Another day, I may ask them to dialogue about a topic in science, math, or social studies, or to record and discuss their responses to a literature selection. They may also be expected to share things they wonder about, questions they have, hopes, dreams, fears—the list is endless. No matter what the subject, the vehicle is written conversation: hearing your partner and responding thoughtfully.

■ Steps and Procedures for Dialogue Journals

Dialogue journals or conversational logs can be started on the first day of school or at any point during the year. Often, teachers begin dialogue journals as teacher-to-student writing, then release the activity to writing partnerships once children are confident and clear about the task. The initial teacher modeling helps writers to be clear about the task and expectations. Dialogue journals are a simple strategy, easily implemented with minimal expense or time. Teachers provide journal materials and simple guidelines depending on purposes they have set, then writers begin! Journal materials might include each child's notebook (partners take turns writing in each other's journal) and shared dialogue journals created and used exclusively by a writing partnership.

No matter how this strategy is implemented, it is important to model appropriate behaviors and provide consistent support for children's efforts and collaboration. Teachers should check in with partners often, then plan further instruction that supports and encourages all kinds of dialogue. Possible mini-lessons to support students' dialogue journaling might address:

1. the length of each entry
2. the importance of listening to the writer's message and responding
3. the kinds of entries
   - questions
   - responses to questions
   - content-specific conversations
4. expectations about language (respectful, no profanities, etc.)
5. asking the writer to "say more"
6. writing for the reader (attention to one's audience).

Teachers should also make clear whether they will read or grade journal entries and what their expectations are in terms of proofreading, correct or working spellings, mechanics, and overall presentation.

Dialogue journals provide a wonderful opportunity for flexibility in pairing writers. Teachers may have students dialogue with their regular writing buddies or allow students to pair spontaneously. Pairing may also vary depending on the task, subject area, and expectations.

◼ Variations and Uses of Dialogue Journals

The uses and types of dialogue journals are infinite and arise from the needs of the students, the teacher, and the curriculum. Teachers will certainly wish to develop specific ideas for their students and programs. One caveat: free, conversational writing such as this can be liberating and fun for students, but if overdone or overprogrammed, reflective writing can turn into a chore. Teachers should listen to children, notice how they are responding to this kind of writing, and take cues from them. A few ideas for using dialogue journals are:

1. sharing life experiences (weekends, vacations, daily home life)
2. responding to literature
3. recording science or math phenomena
   - asking questions
   - making hypotheses
   - illustrating thinking

4. sharing and build stories
5. asking BIG questions in social studies
6. converse with younger or older students in the school (this could be a joint activity where two buddies in one room write to two buddies in another, or a cross-age partnership).

Resources for writers may relate to content or offer stimuli for this type of writing. At the very least, partners will need journals and writing implements. An excellent teacher resource for ideas about dialogue and other types of reflective writing is Fulwiler's (1987) *The Journal Book*. Examples of written correspondence such as *The Jolly Postman: Or Other People's Letters* (Ahlberg and Alhberg 1986) and *Yours truly, Goldilocks* (Ada 1998) provide children with gleeful connections to familiar stories as well as engaging models of effective, dialogic communication.

■ Moving Toward Independence

Like echo writing, dialogue journals are, by definition, a collaborative, peer-to-peer or adult-to-child activity. This kind of reflective writing serves "many purposes, including affective, pragmatic, intellectual, and academic. It is known to improve writing fluency, stimulate cognitive growth, reinforce learning, and foster problem solving skills" (Samway 2006, 138). Such benefits do not cease when writers compose independently. Writers bring the skills, strategies, and problem solving learned in partnership to individual writing projects.

When responding to literature, individual writers of any age can also engage in self-dialogues. Reflecting on content-area subject matter and considering their lives and experiences in individual writing journals, students ask questions, wonder, hypothesize, predict, conclude, and analyze text and experiences. Their reflections became richer and more elaborate after dialoguing with peers.

■ Suggestions for English Language Learners

The use of dialogue journals encourages all learners, to write more elaborately and expansively with less attention to mechanics—particularly those learning English as a second language (Samway 2006). The open-ended content of dialogue journals exposes English language learners to vocabulary and concepts in a relaxed, conversational context that supports language acquisition.

Since this type of journaling is usually much freer, teachers may want to allow cross-code writing, where children switch from English to their first language.

This allows children to strengthen written fluency in their first language and to then share this with peers. Other suggestions for English language learners would be to encourage them to:

- Write dialogue journals at home with parents, siblings, and caregivers.
- Use illustrations and visuals to support and illuminate written entries.
- Use different formats in journals, such as
    - lists
    - diagrams
    - maps.

As preparation for dialoguing, teachers might also pair English language learners with native speakers for some echo writing (see Chapter 8) and allow cross-code writing as children become comfortable with collaboration.

10 Supportive Listeners: Partners as Audience and Editing Buddies

I say to them [her students], "Tell your story to a partner. Make sure it has all the elements of a good story. Read [the story] to your partner . . . use your buddy as a sounding board."

—Sharon Roberts, first-grade teacher

CLASSROOM CHALLENGE

How do I help self-centered, inward focused writers to consider audience, and how do I encourage students to be active, enthusiastic revisers and responsible proofreaders of their work and that of their peers?

■ Supportive Listeners and Editing Buddies: What Are They?

All writers need time and opportunities to develop their listening and editing skills with a trusted partner. When a writer is ready to share a draft of his writing, a supportive listener/editing buddy is there to act as a caring, first audience for this unpolished writing. Editing buddies meet as needed. Some of their roles are to:

- listen
- ask questions
- offer feedback

- guide and suggest strategies to strengthen peers' writing
- offer positive encouragement to fellow writers throughout writing process
- help their partner to complete editing checklists that may then form the basis for discussion

While many children are naturally good listeners and editing buddies, others are not and need explicit teaching and modeling to be effective in these critical roles.

■ Strategy in Action

Jenny Baumeister gathers her first graders on the carpet, instructing them to sit next to their writing buddies. On the wall nearby are her "writing buddy rules." This chart had been created with the children during interactive writing.

Jenny's Writing Buddy Rules Chart
- Be a good leener [learner]
- Face your buddy
- Libry voices
- Pay attnshun
- Give good compliments [this word had been corrected with correction tape]
- No fooling around
- Put your thumb down if it dosit make sense
- Help your writing buddy become a better writer

Jenny reminds students of what a "good writing conference looks like" and talks about their goals as writers. She asks a student, Betsy, to help her demonstrate. Jenny and Betsy model how to conference with each other using a story that Jenny has written on chart paper.

Jenny's Story
On Saturday, I went sledding. We drove there. We had two sleds. We had hot chocolate. We went down the hill four times. One time was very icy. Then, I went another time. Then we came home.

Jenny and Betsy demonstrate supportive, helpful partner behaviors such as asking good questions without giving negative feedback. At several points, Jenny whispers ideas to Betsy, suggesting things she might say. Here is their conversation.

Betsy: What's the most important part of the story?

Jenny: (*asks the children to turn and talk to each other about what they think is the most important part*)

Jenny: Who's the boss of this piece?

Child 1: You are [the writer].

Jenny: That's right. No matter what ideas a partner might have, the writer is always the boss of her writing. (*identifies what is the most important part of her piece and whispers to Betsy*)

Betsy: Can you tell me more?

Jenny: (*elaborates about the "icy part," the section she has identified as most important, by using lots of detail and description, then whispers to Betsy*)

Betsy: You could add that to your story.

Throughout her modeling and discussion, Jenny continually steps back to reinforce and point out what is happening. She creates the following sequence of steps for buddy-writing conferencing:

1. Ask your partner if you can read the writing.
2. Read the writing.
3. Ask what's the most important part.
4. Talk about it together.

Students then disperse with buddies to begin sharing writing pieces. I check in with Tony and Carl who are sitting side by side at a table, conferring over Tony's story.

Tony	**Carl**
[points] That's lowercase	
	[points] That's uppercase.

Jenny checks in and asks Carl what was the most important part of Tony's story. She converses with Carl about what he thinks Tony might add or delete. Jenny then reads Tony's story aloud, praising his "great lead." She asks for the class' attention and shares Tony's "great beginning" with everyone.

Tony	**Carl**
[*reads Carl's story aloud*]	
The important part was . . . you said—	
	The chocolate part!
Okay . . . you could add . . . like . . . ummm . . . like umm . . . where were you?	
	In the den?

You could add that. If you forget,
   it's okay.
You could write that [*points to Carl's paper*]
Or, you could add that [*points again*]
Or like the other?

Partners continue, listening and talking for about twenty minutes until Jenny calls them together to share.

Jenny's students are surrounded by helpful charts about literacy and collaboration that they have created together. Titles include:

- Rules for Reading Buddies
- Rules for Writing Buddies
- Editing Checklists
- Writers' Tools
- Getting Our Minds Ready to Read/Write
- Writing Small Moments
- Writing Strong Leads
- Writers Revise
- A Writing Teacher's Job

Jenny's is a classroom with a strong daily focus on literacy. Her classroom is also a space that has been created and defined with children, not introduced to them after the fact.

Ownership is hugely important in building academic communities where learners are engaged, motivated, risk takers, and eager, responsive problem solvers. Jenny has obviously built the environment with this group of children so that classroom walls are viewed as resources that writing buddies continually make use of to support their planning, composing, editing, and revising.

■ Minilessons for Supportive Listening and Effective Editing

Addressing editing and the role of the listener or audience should be a regular, routine aspect of the minilessons preceding partner writing. Teachers develop minilessons based on:

- their learning objectives for students as editors and listeners
- the needs of curriculum and writing program
- their observations of what editing skills and strategies writers need as they check in and confer with writing partnerships

As Jenny and Betsy demonstrate in the minilesson, teachers can model and instruct the role of supportive listener and editing buddy simultaneously. While students and context will determine the subject of minilessons for each classroom, here are a few minilesson ideas to get you started.

1. *Listening, editing, revising, and publishing.* The teacher and students develop a framework or structure *together*, so that writing partners are well acquainted with expectations. Make sure the expectations, frameworks, guidelines, and structures you develop are
   - written down
   - posted prominently on classroom walls and
   - available to writing partners as individual copies.

2. *Teacher-student-prompted demonstration.* The teacher decides on an objective for the minilesson—in Jenny's case, asking good questions as a "Writing Teacher"—then prompts the student writer with appropriate language and questioning strategies. Possible topics for teacher-prompted minilessons would be:
   - how to be a supportive listener
     - Use supportive listening behaviors (eye contact, position in relation to the writer).
     - Use supportive responses that go beyond "good job."
     - Focus on the writer and what she is trying to express.
   - asking appropriate questions
   - how to be a "Writing Teacher"
   - helping the writer identify important parts of a piece
   - helping the writer to say more
   - reminding the writer about classroom resources and helping him to locate them.

3. *Student-to-student modeling and demonstration.* The teacher identifies a partnership that is effectively using editing or listening strategies and skills or has developed new, effective strategies, behaviors, or language and asks them to demonstrate these to the whole class.

4. *Tools and resources for editing buddies.* The teacher gives explicit instruction in how to use a particular editing tool. Examples include:
   - an editing checklist
   - a revising questions form
   - a peer response form.

No matter what minilessons we provide for writing buddies, we want to revisit skills and strategies taught frequently.

Appropriate Questioning

Children continually amaze me with the kinds of questioning they use with each other when conferring over writing. Their ideas are often right on target and much more helpful to their writing buddy than those I have suggested. There are a number of reasons for this, but two stand out:

- *Experience.* In ongoing, long-term writing partnerships, children get to know each other's interests, strengths, weaknesses, and needs better than anyone, including the teacher.
- *Developmental proximity.* Understanding another's needs at any given moment may be enhanced when learners work with peers closest to them in development.

Here are some questions I have heard students use and teachers model for listening and editing buddies.

Teacher and Peer Questions

- What's the most important part? Why? Can you say more about this?
- What is your argument?
- What are your reasons for your argument?
- What is your supporting evidence for your reasons?
- What are the basic assumptions or values behind your argument? (Brady and Jacobs 1994)
- Can you point to a place in your story where you "show" rather than "tell"?
- Where will you go from here?
- Did rereading your story to me give you an idea about something you might want to change?

Tools and Resources for Listening and Editing Buddies

Editing checklists, revising forms, and peer response forms are three commonly used tools for partners, but there are many others we can apply in the partnerships process depending on children's age, development, writing genre, task, and many other considerations. There are also many excellent teacher resources that help students become supportive listeners and effective editing collaborators. See the resource list at the end of the chapter for a few of my favorites.

Editing Checklists   Editing is a very different process than writing whether we undertake it alone or with a buddy. Students need to understand this distinction

and the value of supportive editing in ultimately getting them where they need to be as writers—in meeting grade-level expectations (Davis and Hill 2003) and in writing effectively and clearly for a particular audience. In most classrooms I visit, teachers use some sort of developmentally appropriate checklist for individual writers' use in editing. These checklists may be from published resources or textbooks or developed by a team of school or district teachers. Sometimes teachers use school, district, or state guidelines to frame a discussion of editing with their students, out of which comes a student-designed checklist.

No matter what type of checklist a teacher uses with individual writers, there is often the opportunity to modify and adapt this form with students for use in writing partnerships. A completed Partners Editing Checklist is shown in Figure 10–1 and a blank form can be found in Appendix D. Teachers are encouraged to develop their own forms that suit their students' age, developmental level, and writing needs.

Revising or Questioning Form   I am always inspired and awed by Georgia Heard's advice to writers and teachers of writers. The idea for a "revising or questioning form" comes from her "peer conferring revision questions" (Heard 2002, 114). Different from editing checklists, revising or questioning forms give students a language to use in talking with partners about a piece of writing. The

WE EDIT: PARTNERS EDITING CHECKLIST

NAMES _Gina_ (1) _Kayla_ (2)

TITLE _Guess What I Am_ WRITER _Kayla_

GENRE _Poem_ DATE _10/4/06_

	WRITERS	
SPELLING	1	2

I/we...

- Found words that don't look right ✓ ☐
- Checked for "tricky words" ✓ ☐
- Used the dictionary or other resource ✓ ☐

Comments _Everything was spelled correctly and there were no tricky words used in-correctly._

DOES IT MAKE SENSE?

I/we...

- Checked to see if words or parts were missing ✓ ☐
- Checked sentences – were they too long? Confusing? ✓ ☐
- Read and retold to the writer to make sure of understanding ✓ ☐

Comments _Everything made sense and everything was in perfect form of a sentence but a poem form._

PUNCTUATION

I/we ...

- Checked for **periods, commas, question marks** and **exclamation marks** ✓ ☐
- Checked for **upper case letters** to begin each sentence, and proper nouns ✓ ☐

Comments _Need to add commas at the end of a thought and exclamation marks at the end of the poem_

OTHER EDITING CONSIDERATIONS

I/we...

- Checked for indented paragraphs ✓ ☐
- Checked for legible handwriting ✓ ☐
- Discussed what was needed before publishing ✓ ☐

Comments _Needs to indent at the beginning on a paragraph._

FIG. 10–1 *Editing Buddies Checklist*

ultimate purpose of such talk is revision, but the deeper value, in my opinion, lies in helping learners step back and really see themselves as writers engaged in a dynamic process of crafting a piece of writing. Borrowing from Heard's work, a possible revising and questioning format is offered here, but, again, teachers are encouraged to adapt, change, and modify it to suit their classroom's of writers.

Revising and Questioning Form

What can the writer tell me?

1. How can I help you?
2. What should I be listening for?
3. Why did you choose to write this piece?
4. Did your idea work out when you wrote it down?
5. What was easy about writing this piece?
6. What was difficult? Can I help with this?
7. What are the most important parts of this piece? Is there more you can tell me about these parts?
8. What is your plan for this piece?
9. What is your plan for your next piece?

It is important to emphasize that the revising and questioning form is a tool for *partner discussion*, not another fill-in-the-blank activity. Teachers can enlarge the form as a chart posted on the classroom wall, laminate it for partners to grab when needed, or keep it as a resource in writing folders. Wherever forms are housed, having them readily available ensures that writing partners will use them during editing and revising times. Finally, it is important to provide time for partners to share how their editing conversation went, how they used forms, and what additional questions or discussion points they employed.

Peer Response Forms   Like checklists and revising forms, peer response sheets vary according to the age development, and needs of writers and the genre of writing. A reproducible form can be found in Appendix D, but clearly responses will vary widely depending on task and criteria. Like revising and questioning forms, peer response forms provide important catalysts for discussion. They also provide the writer with valuable written feedback, which she can refer to as she revises.

Writing partners need modeling and instruction in how to effectively use peer response forms. They are not meant to be something a buddy completes and hands to her partner without discussion. Teachers will want to outline procedures for partners to follow, such as:

- When to use a peer response form
- Process of completing the form
    - The editor should ask the writer to read the piece aloud.
    - The editor needs a copy of the piece before completing the form.

- How to share the contents of the form with the writer
  - Share each response verbally.
  - Discuss each response.
  - Discuss possible follow-up questions or responses.
  - Expand responses beyond "suggested responses" and criteria outlined.
  - Give time for the writer to ask questions or elaborate.
- How to hand over response form to writer
- Follow-up discussions (before, during, or after revision)

The procedures described here, as well as many similar ones teachers use, are designed to deepen learners' awareness of their own writing process, to help them to learn from each other and to step back from writing—their own and their partner's—and to focus explicitly on all aspects of process. As writing teachers, we always want to remember that it is not the tools and forms we give partners, but the writing itself that matters.

■ Moving Toward Independence

As children become supportive listeners and editing buddies for one another, they internalize editing and revising tools, strategies, and skills, which they apply to individual writing projects. After practicing and refining editing skills with a supportive peer, individuals are much clearer about teacher expectations for editing and revision, and more confident in their ability to take a second, third, or fourth look at their writing.

In moving children toward independence teachers may want to keep the following progression in mind:

1. Teacher and group teach, and model, guided practice of the strategy.
2. Partners practice strategy.
3. Partners share their experiences with the whole class.
4. Teacher reteaches and models the strategy for individual writers.
5. Students use the strategy with independent writing pieces.
6. Individuals share experiences with the whole class.

■ Suggestions for English Language Learners

When working with students learning English, writing teachers should focus on content first, with the awareness that mechanics—spelling, grammar, punctuation, and usage—will come later with students' greater exposure to oral and written English. This awareness is something teachers must also convey to partners of English language learners.

Young readers and writers frequently tell me that they assist their partners with mechanics, sounding out when reading and spelling when writing. This focus may be the result of a number of factors, such as the greater visibility of mechanical errors, their mimicking what teachers or instructional texts emphasize, or the emphasis many parents and caregivers place on this aspect of literacy. It is up to teachers to shift partners' focus away from mechanics and toward some of the skills and strategies at the heart of writing—content, voice, organization, and fluency. While the listening and editing strategies in this chapter are focused on these areas, teachers of English language learners might consider specific teaching and *reteaching* of strategies for English language learners and their partners.

■ Resources

There are many wonderful books to guide teachers of K through 6 writers today. A few of my favorites are listed here. Many contain checklists and buddy responses forms appropriate for writing partners of all ages. They also offer a wealth of strategies and helpful suggestions for supporting children's writing in all genres.

CALKINS, L. M. 1994. *The Art of Teaching Writing.*

DAVIS, J., AND S. HILL. 2003. *The No-Nonsense Guide to Teaching Writing: Strategies, Structures and Solutions.*

FLETCHER. R. 1993. *What a Writer Needs.*

FLETCHER, R., AND J. PORTALUPI. 1998. *Craft Lessons: Teaching Writing, K–8.*

HARWAYNE, S. 2001. *Writing Through Childhood: Rethinking Process and Product.*

ROUTMAN, R. 2000. *Conversations: Strategies for Teaching, Learning, and Evaluating.*

SPANDEL, V. 2001. *Books, Lessons, Ideas for Teaching the Six Traits: Writing in the Elementary and Middle Grades.*

ZINSSER, W. 1976. *On Writing Well: An Informal Guide to Writing Non-Fiction.*

Writing-Fluency Buddies

11

I choose [to write with] a partner because you get more ideas. You prob'ly write longer paragraphs [when it's] not just your ideas, [but] both. If you get stuck, you ask your partner instead of asking the teacher.

—Third grader

CLASSROOM CHALLENGE

How can I provide peer support for short-term writing projects and goals?

■ Writing-Fluency Buddies: What Are They?

Writing-Fluency Buddy time provides collaborative opportunities for writers to co-compose quick, structured pieces demonstrating skills and strategies learned during direct instruction. It also allows for "mixing up" students, so writers work with many peers during the course of the year. Writing-fluency buddies typically work together for a brief period of time—usually a week—practicing a specific skill or strategy that has been explicitly taught to them at a particular time. Unlike most writing partnerships where students are paired for a longer time period or for the duration of a particular writing project, fluency buddies are paired briefly for short-term practice.

■ Missy's Writers

On a mid-December morning, Missy Taylor's second graders are co-composing acrostic poems about holiday traditions. Missy explains the activity, then writing fluency buddies disperse around the classroom, decide who will scribe first, and begin completing their poems. I check in with Haley and Anne. Haley is scribing while Anne watches, offering ideas and editing suggestions. They have decided to switch scribing with each line of the poem. After several minutes of conversation and consulting a "holiday word list" Missy has distributed, Anne writes the first line, "T."

Anne	**Haley**
[*writes*] **T***rees whisper*	
while the awtaments [ornaments] sway.	
	My turn. [*takes the pen*]
Riding?	
	Yup, they could be on a sleigh.
Riding on a sleigh?	
	Santa comes to . . .
cheer the day!	
	What about "cheer up" the day?
[*nods*] Okay.	
	[*writes*] **R***ideing on a slay Santa comes to cheer up the day.* [*hands the pen to Anne*]

They spend several minutes discussing what they might possibly write for the letter *A*. They consult the holiday word list and classroom word wall and then scan the classroom walls. Finally, they ask me for an idea and I suggest they might start their sentence with the word *A*.

Anne	**Haley**
A snowflake!	
	What does it do?
Dances?	
	and twirls?
A snowflake dances and twirls	
around while listening to . . .	the Christmas . . .
sound! [*writes*] **A** *snowflake dances and twerls around while lisning to the Christmas sound.*	

As I move away to observe other writers, Anne and Haley decide to skip D and work on *I* as Haley has suggested they write about "icicles." After fifteen minutes, Missy brings the writers together to share their pieces.

Missy provided a quick explanation of the task, sent writing-fluency buddies off, and, when wrapping up her lesson, brought them together to share. This writing activity lends itself to instant or flexible grouping where the main purpose is to get children writing quickly and fluently. It is brief, the structure is clear, and it can be used with new or experienced writing partners.

Steps and Procedures

In general, writing-fluency buddies are paired for one week. While teachers will want to adapt this strategy to suit the needs of their program and students, a general sequence for writing fluency buddies might be as follows:

1. The teacher models and teaches a specific skill or strategy.
2. The teacher explains expectations for partner work.
3. The students work together for short periods each day (ten to fifteen minutes) with their writing-fluency buddy.
4. The students share their work with the entire class later in the week.

Again, the emphasis is on *short, focused practice* of specific skills. Writing-fluency buddies do not engage in long-term collaborations, but work together to practice and reach deeper understanding and facility with specific skills and strategies.

Minilessons and Ideas

There are a myriad of writing skills, strategies, and tasks on which a teacher might ask fluency buddies to focus. This is a framework that must adapt to grade-level curriculum and expectations. In a short, focused piece of writing, fluency buddies might work together to practice:

- varying sentence length
- using different kinds of sentences—statements, questions, and exclamations
- using appropriate text signals to signify meaning, voice, and tone
  - using punctuation—periods, commas, question marks, exclamation points, quotation (or "talking") marks, semicolons, hyphens, dashes, colons, etc.
  - using bold capitalized and italicized text

- using rhyme
- using repetition—experimenting with the effect of repeating a word or phrase
- creating unique voices for each character in a story
- showing, not telling
- recognizing each other's voice and style
- experimenting with voice and style
- incorporating a particular text structure, or several such as cause and effect or compare and contrast into a piece
- writing a paragraph with main idea and supporting details
- writing like "an author."

Quickwrites

Creating five-minute quickwrites (see Figure 11–1) exercises partners' writing muscles and encourages spontaneous, fluent writing. Students can decide whether to expand their piece or use the quickwrite as a warm-up activity for a self-selected writing activity. Procedures for "quickwrites" are as follows:

1. Partners read the quickwrite prompt.
2. Partners check the timer (they may want to designate one person as the timer, but that person should also write).
3. Partners write their own pieces for five minutes.
4. Partners read quickwrites to one another and decide whether to expand one or both.

Since this activity is designed to encourage writing fluency, it is important that each child write. Teachers use many prompts for "quickwrites." Some of my favorites come from Regie Routman (2000):

- Next year, I plan to . . .
- I remember when . . .
- One time I . . .
- Yesterday I . . .
- I never knew . . .
- A long time ago I . . . (this is my absolute; favorite; it elicits wonderful pieces from kindergartners *and* my college students!)
- I was surprised . . .
- I noticed . . .

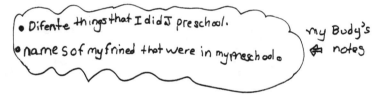

FIG. 11–1   *Student Quickwrite Sample and Buddy Suggestion*

- I wish . . .
- I don't understand why . . . (216)

■ Moving Toward Independence

Once a writer practices a particular skill or strategy with her writing fluency buddy, she can use it more confidently and comfortably when crafting independent writing pieces. Often teachers offer structures and guidelines when teaching a particular skill or strategy. These guidelines, outlining expectations and task criteria, can be posted on classroom walls or copied and given to writers to use in independent writing.

■ Suggestions for English Language Learners

English language learners benefit from access to many models of English speaking, clear expectations, and explicit structures for completing writing tasks. Short-term writing fluency partnerships provide continual access to all three. Additionally, writing fluency partnerships for English language learners should include visual reminders, and reteaching.

Buddy Writing Centers 12

If the teacher chooses the buddies, it's not always that fun. When I go to center [Buddy Writing Center], I choose . . . if it's your friend and you have a silly buddy, you still have some time left to do your work.

—Second grader

CLASSROOM CHALLENGE

How can I find more time and choice for students wanting to partner up for writing?

Mike Rose (1989) writes that "writing and reading are such private acts that we forget how fundamentally social they are: We hear stories read by others and we like to tell others about the stories we read; we learn to write from others and we write for others to read us" (109–118). Much of children's school life involves solitary acts of reading and writing, independent projects, and assessments of individuals achievement. On the other hand, the "real world" is all about collaboration. In business and academia, adults meet to collaborate, discuss, and write. One way to replicate these real-world contexts is to create literacy centers where students come together to collaborate over reading or writing. Buddy writing centers allow students choice about when to partner up and with whom.

■ Minilessons for Getting Centers Started

As when implementing a classroom learning center, teachers should make center rules, routines, and expectations clear, then allow all students to practice and familiarize themselves with routines and activities *before opening the center for independent work.* Minilessons or instructions on starting centers would address the following:

- number of writers allowed
- use and care of center materials
- setup and cleanup procedures
- working procedures
  - voice volume
  - sharing the writing
  - working through challenges or difficulties.

Once general procedures are clear, teachers may change writing activities weekly, monthly, or as often as needed. They may also have "free days" when center buddies choose what kind of writing they want to do. Since center work is largely independent, teachers may want to use this time for students to revisit or practice familiar kinds of writing.

■ Space and Materials

Buddy writing centers may have a designated space—a table, desks, or countertop—or be movable, with materials and supplies in bins, folders, cupboards, vertical files, baskets, or "writing buckets" as Cheryl Feeney uses with her second graders. With portable writing centers, writers can settle on the spot in the classroom that is most comfortable for them.

Materials for buddy writing centers might include, but are not limited to the following:

- buddy writing folders
- crayons, pencils, pens, markers
- writing journals
- "seed journals" for partners' writing ideas (Second-grade teacher Cheryl Feeney uses tiny "seed journals," which her students often take home to brainstorm ideas for writing with their parents. They move from students' homework folders to desks and the writing bucket)
- dictionaries—with or without pictures—thesauruses
- writers' word books (where writers keep lists of words they would like to use in their writing)
- editing and revising checklists
- writing prompts
- various types of paper

- guidelines for a particular activity
- "old favorites" for partners to use on free-choice days

■ Ideas and Minilessons for Buddy Writing Centers

As mentioned earlier, partners may revisit old favorites or practice familiar writing activities in centers where extra time and experience builds their confidence as collaborators and independent writers. Once general procedures, rules, and routines are established, teachers' instruction for center buddies would focus on expectations for a particular project or activity. Teachers may want to give minilessons that include the activities presented here.

"Telephone"

This activity is similar to the old telephone listening game, where partners or small groups add to a story, one sentence (or two) at a time. There are many ways to do this activity:

- One buddy writes a sentence or two, then passes the paper.
- One buddy whispers a sentence to his buddy, the next writes what he heard, then they switch.
- Buddies whisper an idea to each other, then each writes what she heard and compare sentences.

Structured Writing Activities

Once modeled and taught whole-class, structured writing activities naturally extend into buddy centers. Basically, writers are provided with a familiar, patterned "structure," which they then use as a support in composing their own original pieces. A few examples of structured writing include, but are not limited to:

1. *Concept or word poems* are created using a simple scaffold such as the one in Figure 12–1. Taking a concept or word such as *night*, partners fill in the blanks to create an instant poem. Ideas for this simple structure are endless. For example, try the words *world, puppies, kittens, storm, snakes, clouds, ocean,* or *earth.* If you stock the center with small sticky notes, writers can play with word order and create different effects, rhythms, and patterns in concept poems.
2. *Buddy poems* are written side by side, with each partner supplying a word for each line. Poems might be written as a response to an experience, a piece of literature, or a shared interest.

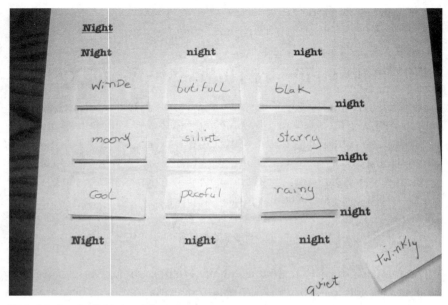

FIG. 12–1 *Scaffolded "Night" Poem*

3. *Pyramid poems* are fun to write and even more fun to read, the momentum building with each line. As the name implies, the poem begins with one word, then two, and so on until the poets decide they have reached the end.

4. *Borrowed poems* come with built-in rhythms, patterns, and tone, which we "borrow" from the poet. Most kindergarten and first-grade teachers have made a "borrowed story" or poem using the wonderfully simple structure of Bill Martin's *Brown Bear, Brown Bear, What Do You See?* (1983). In borrowed poems, partners use the structure of poems and text to create innovations.

5. *People poems* are used to tell students' stories or to explore the lives of historical figures. The structure found in Appendix F is simple and can be varied to suit the age of writers, type of writing project, or subject of the people poem.

It is important *to teach and model* all structured writing ideas *before* offering them as a choice in a buddy writing center.

Character Studies

Teachers can stock buddy writing centers with many literature selections that have strong characterization. Partners read and examine these texts focusing specifically on characters. Character study sheets, such as those in Appendix J can support these explorations.

Alphabet Activities

When choosing alphabet activities, the possibilities are limitless. Partners explore many examples of alphabet books, then create their own. They can also work together on word-family books or embark on word, letter, or sound searches using books found in the center or around the classroom.

Author Studies

As the name implies, partners explore and read from many selections of an author's work. They may also

- Write a response or review of an author's book.
- Mimic the author's style in a jointly composed piece.
- Write an advertisement promoting an author.

Thematic Writing Activities

If a class is studying a particular theme or topic, books that a teacher reads aloud can be placed in a buddy writing center for partners to explore. Partners read from many selections related to a theme, such as friendship or heroes. Joy Moss' (1984, 1990) books *Focus Units in Literature: A Handbook for Elementary School Teachers* and *Focus on Literature: A Context for Literacy Learning* are wonderful resources when planning thematic units. After studying examples of literature on a particular theme, partners may also use center time to co-compose their own variation on the theme. See Chapter 17 for ideas and suggestions for thematic studies.

Genre Writing

As in thematic and author studies, a teacher would stock the buddy writing center with examples of that genre. Partners then explore, read, and discuss in preparation for writing their own co-composed genre piece. If a class is engaged in a genre study, extending this work into a buddy writing center allows students to choose this type of writing again to practice and refine their skills. See Chapter 14 for further exploration of genre writing.

■ Moving Toward Independence

Well-planned buddy writing centers provide writers with the context and support to be successful individual writers. Center activities are usually familiar to students. Centers provide time and space for children to practice and refine skills with the social support of peers. If a writer of any age learns something through direct instruction and guided practice and is then given time and opportunity to revisit in a buddy writing center, he is that much more confident when later attempting writing independently.

▪ Considerations for English Language Learners

Since center activities are mostly those that writers are revisiting rather than encountering for the first time, they make ideal contexts for English language learners. In the fast-paced world of today's classrooms, teachers move from teaching one skill to the next. In endeavoring to cover the curriculum, they sometimes leave students struggling to learn English in the dust. Affording young writers some breathing room to revisit activities and tasks with which they are familiar, but not necessarily confident, is especially important for ELLs. Additional supports for English language learners' participation in centers include, the following:

- Plan center activities that engage students in multiple linguistic processes (reading, writing, listening, and speaking).
- Provide clear, step-by-step directions with visual cues whenever possible.
- Use tape recorders, books on tape, and other auditory aids to supplement written texts and directions.
- Pay attention to "pairing" and who will make the most supportive writing buddies for center activities (see Chapter 1 for suggestions about compatible pairing).

▪ Concluding Thoughts

Buddy writing centers provide children with the opportunity to practice and revisit favorite writing projects and activities. If a classroom has "center time," students who enjoy collaborating over writing can choose this bonus time to co-compose a wide variety of texts. If the center is open during "free" writing time, writers may choose to buddy-up in center to work on pieces in progress. Such work might entail taking notes, researching, and writing a first draft. Or partners may want to use the time to edit and revise their work with a peer. Some children love to collaborate; others do not. Allowing them a choice by making a buddy writing center a part of classroom life responds to the diverse needs of all learners at any age.

Community Messages: Writing with an Audience and Purpose in Mind

13

I'm always questioning them about audience, nudging them to ask themselves questions like, "Would kindergartners be interested in this?" Writing for readers is our purpose here.

—Sharon Roberts, first-grade teacher

CLASSROOM CHALLENGE

How do I transition my students from the highly teacher-controlled activities of interactive and modeled writing to greater independence as writers?

■ Community Messages: What Are They?

Community messages are short, informational texts written for a specific audience. First-grade teacher Sharon Roberts uses community messages to naturally extend her program's interactive, shared, or modeled writing activities; however, teachers can use community messages to model purposeful writing for specific audiences of any grade. Topics for such messages could be:

- classroom events, special projects, or announcements
- upcoming schoolwide events

- calendar reminders (such as Groundhog Day)
- information about a topic children are studying
- invitations to performances or class events

The content of community messages is determined by the children, class, and school.

▪ Strategy in Action

Sharon Roberts' first graders are in a circle, sitting beside their writing buddy at the start of writers workshop. Once the children are settled, Sharon calls their attention to the Partner Writing Chart (Figure 13–1). Hanging beside the Partner Writing Chart, is a Partner Reading Chart (Figure 13–2). Sharon began partner writing in January as an extension of interactive writing, but her students have been buddy reading since the first week of school.

Sharon asks the children to suggest possible writing topics for the day's community messages. The children suggest the following:

- Groundhog Day
- a calendar change from January to February

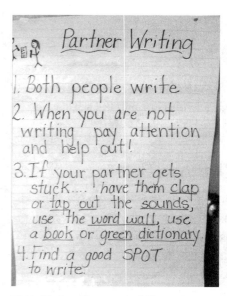

FIG. 13–1   *Sharon's Rule for Writing Partners Chart*

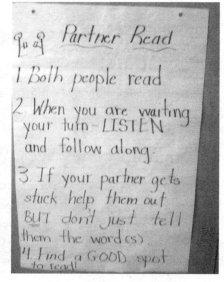

FIG. 13–2   *Sharon's Rule for Reading Partners Chart*

- the assembly
- the classroom visitor (I was observing the class)
- Officer Dan, a police officer due to talk with them about safety
- people absent from class

Then Sharon addresses the group.

Sharon: Okay, everyone find a spot. Talk to your partner about what you want to write about. Once you've decided and negotiated on your topic, raise your hand and I'll bring you paper, markers, and correction tape.

The children disperse and discuss what they will write about. Nan and Billy raise their hand. When Sharon arrives, they tell her they've settled on two topics—Groundhog Day and the assembly. Sharon hands them a large sheet of white construction paper, black markers, and an eight-inch strip of correction tape.

Sharon says, "Okay, do you know how you're going to put these two ideas together? Good—get right to work."

Billy	**Nan**
[*writes*] *January 13 2006.*	
	That's not the 13th [*draws a circle around the date, covers with correction tape, then writes*] *January 31, 2006.*
[*draws a line down the left side of the paper to use as their "have a go space"*]	
	Okay, now we can write, team!
[*writes*] *in today it is* [*hands the marker to Nan*]	
	[*practices in the "have a go space" space*] *grown* [*then she returns to main body of the message and writes*] *grownday.* Okay, are we done?
[*reads the sentence and recognizes that "grownday" is missing "hog"*]	

Nan places correction tape over *grownday* and writes *grownhogday*. She, then writes a plus sign, before hopping up to check the day's schedule to see if they have Assembly.

Another partnership, Ellie and Ken sit nearby. They are working on the second sentence of their story, also about Groundhog Day. Ellie has acted as scribe for the first sentence and then hands Ken the marker.

Ken	Ellie
[*writes*] *in two days, it's . . .* [*pauses before writing Groundhog Day*]	
	[*takes marker*] It's a "g" [*writes*] *g*. Oh, I need to write an uppercase letter.

At this moment, Sharon checks in. She says, "Is it the name of a specific holiday?" Ellie and Ken nod and Ellie applies correction tape and writes, *G*. She then asks Sharon for help spelling *groundhog*. Sharon encourages her to use the have-a-go space to "write the parts you know."

Ellie: (working in the have-a-go space, writes) hog . . . grownhog . . .
Sharon: What else could say, "ow"?
Ellie: "ʊ"? *(writes) grundhog.*
Sharon: Anything else?
Ellie: (adds "o" before "u," returns to message, and writes) Groundhog day.

Children continue writing for approximately twenty-five minutes. At the end of the writers' workshop, Sharon gathers partners on the carpet and asks each partnership what resources they used. Children offer many ideas—word wall, green dictionaries, calendar, stories hanging on the walls, and their previous writing pieces. Sharon then asks Ken and Ellie to share how they worked through the spelling of Groundhog Day. Ellie responds, "We did *hog*" cause we know *dog*.

This leads to a short discussion led by Sharon, with contributions by several children, about using sounds we know, like *ow*, to think about other sounds, like *ou*. Sharon concludes by saying, "We should work from things we know to those we want to know but don't." She then calls students' attention to partners who have written their message in the form of a list. After asking these writers to read their lists, she praises them for selecting this structure to make their meaning clear. Another pair reads their story and Sharon asks if the list form of writing would have worked for their piece. They shake their heads. Sharon says, "That's okay. Sometimes things work for one writer or partnership and one kind of writing, but not for another."

Reading community messages continues until each partnership has read their piece aloud. After each reading, Sharon points to a strength of the piece of writing, highlights the children's use of resources, and asks them to explain their process. Once pieces are completed—usually by the end of the day—they are delivered to designated readers around the school building.

The level of "strategy talk" in Sharon Roberts' room is truly remarkable. She uses a high level of literate language, and her students' talk reflects this. Every Tuesday, partners compose community messages. Sharon's careful structuring of these interactions through minilessons, modeling, discussion, reminder charts, and rules for buddy writing ensure that these collaborations are effective and support students' developing writing skills and strategies.

For Sharon's first graders, the shift from interactive writing as the year progressed was a step toward writing independence. With writing partnerships, however, as teachers cede responsibility to children, individual writers are not left completely on their own. With a peer at their side, writers are supported and guided. Partnerships become bridges between teacher-directed, guided writing work and completely independent writing.

For older students, who are expected to write fluently in many subject areas—math and science journals and reports, narratives, poems, reading responses, social studies reports, book reports, prompted writing in preparation for state testing, and a myriad of other tasks—community messages can offer a welcome "break in the action." These short, manageable pieces of purposeful writing help partners and individuals focus on writing for a reader. As students ask critical questions, they tailor writing for specific and varied reading audiences.

■ Steps and Procedures for Getting Started

Steps and procedures for introducing and using community messages depend on the ages of writers and audiences for whom they are composing. Each teacher will want to modify and adapt the strategy as needed. Suggestions for getting started include:

- identifying the audience and the purpose for writing
- modeling appropriate partner procedures and expectations through minilessons and group discussions
- identifying the specific instructional goals and skills to be addressed in a community message lesson

Identifying the Audience and Purposes for Writing

The community messages snapshots at the beginning of the chapter occurred in January, about three weeks after Sharon began her writing partnerships. When introducing writing partnerships, Sharon initially focuses lessons on the skills necessary for effective collaboration; however, by mid-February, and for the remainder of the year, Sharon's students write their community messages for specific, pre-selected audiences. Partners work together to tailor writing pieces for their readers, a challenging but appropriate undertaking for first graders the second half of the year, when skills and writing fluency are stronger.

Identifying an audience may be as simple as asking other classes or individual teachers and building administrators to be the receivers of weekly messages. Community messages can also be sent to local businesses, civic organizations, newspapers. The key is finding receptive, accessible audiences for this writing. Sometimes writers receive responses to their messages, but this is not necessary; the point is to focus on writers' collaboration. The possibilities for audiences are endless. Teachers and students should brainstorm possible audiences, then consider writing for their chosen readers. Possible audiences for weekly community messages include, but are not limited to:

- other classes in the school
- the school principal or other administrators
- special-subject teachers (art, music, PE, etc.)
- students and classes in other district schools or those in a neighboring district
- local politicians
- community members (fire, police, etc.)

- local businesses
- local newspapers

Remember, the most important thing is to support writers' collaboration as they create messages for particular readers. The sooner you identify recipients for community messages, the sooner partners can begin!

Modeling Appropriate Partner Procedures and Expectations

A quick review of expectations should precede minilessons about community messages. Most teachers post rules for writing partners and remind students about them regularly, adding a new rule or guideline as needed. Reminders might specify that each partner writes, contributes ideas, pays attention, or helps find appropriate writing resources. Reminders should always include a discussion of audience. Depending on the audience, the purpose of the message, and the genre of writing, writing partners may address more specific and critical questions as they begin composing their community message. A few questions might be:

- Why are we writing this message to this audience or reader(s) at this point in time?
- How do we need to adapt, change, or tailor our writing for this audience?
- How can we structure this writing so that these readers will be interested or will understand?
- Will kindergartners understand this recipe we want to share with them?
- Can we be clearer?
- Will illustrations help?
- Is there a particular format or structure that will make our message clearer?
- Is the purpose of our message to inform, ask, invite, entertain, etc.?

Identifying the Specific Instructional Goals and Skills to be Addressed in a Community Message Lesson

Community messages are quick, fun, and satisfying for students of all ages. They are also important elements of a comprehensive literacy program. To this end, teachers should have a specific instructional focus for these lessons. In the snapshots that began this chapter, Sharon Robert's focus for partners is "finding and using resources." Sharon makes this focus explicit to writers during pre- and post-writing activities as well as when she confers with each partnership. This is critical.

Teachers might choose to introduce a new skill, concept, or strategy for writers to use in the writing of a community message, then later, during direct instruction and guided practice, provide practice or reinforcement. Alternatively, teachers might use community message writing as a vehicle for students to practice and reinforce skills, concepts, and writing techniques previously taught. Whatever the focus, it should be clearly stated to students: "Now, let's talk about resources"; "Remember to include transition words in your piece."

Possible minilesson themes preceding community message writing include:

- writing a summary
- finding and using writing resources (reference books, spelling journals, classroom walls, word walls, dictionaries, thesauruses, and the Internet)
- using topic sentences and supporting details to build strong paragraphs
- using transition words effectively
- choosing the appropriate structure or format for a particular message—T-charts, Venn diagrams, lists, narrative structure, webs, bold, colorful print, etc.
- developing a clear, consistent writing voice
- sharing across partnerships or rehearsing with a practice audience before delivering the community message.

◼ Moving Toward Independence

Jointly composing community messages is so much fun for all ages that the activity often takes on a life of its own. Enthused individual writers often take the initiative to identify audiences to whom they would like to write on their own. Students also write messages to each other, students in other classrooms and schools, community members, authors, parents, and others. The practice of deliberately considering the audience in short, focused bits of writing helps individual writers consider the reader more carefully in other types of independent writing, whether narrative, nonfiction, notes, rules, charts, informational flyers about upcoming classroom events, or even responses to literature.

◼ Considerations for English Language Learners

The almost continuous conversation involved in composing community messages presents many opportunities for students to develop oral and written language proficiencies with specific purposes and real-life applications in mind. Here are some strategies that enhance and support English language learners' involvement:

- Introduce relevant vocabulary that writing partners might use for a specific kind of message or audience and provide a list of such vocabulary, either posted on chart paper or distributed as individual resource sheets.
- Model different formats and structures, accompanied with actions and, when appropriate, using labels, captions, and other visuals.
- Provide sufficient sharing time at the close of each lesson for partners to read, reread, and discuss components of their community messages.
- When conferencing with writing partners and during sharing time, pose questions that solicit students' thoughts and decisions about their writing process.
- Encourage writers to accompany their messages with illustrations, captions, and labels.

■ Concluding Thoughts

Community messages are flexible, engaging writing activities for all learners. They may relate to students' lives or to what is engaging attention and interest at a particular moment in time. Younger writers' messages may be shorter and rely more heavily on pictures than those of older writers, but not necessarily. These messages might also include photographs, collages, or pictures clipped from magazines and newspapers. The message's content and format depend on what is to be communicated; the skills and imagination of the writers; and the needs, interests, and reading capabilities of the intended audience. This type of communication is less formal and friendlier than some writing genres. As such, it is an ideal co-composing strategy.

14 | Exploring Genre: Making Reading– Writing Connections

Partners give you information about what to write about and when we read stories, it gives us ideas.

—Second grader

■ Exploring Genre: Making Reading–Writing Connections: What Is It?

As its name implies, making reading and writing connections involves tasks and activities designed for students to make explicit connections between reading and writing through exploration and research into genres of writing, followed by co-composing original, genre-specific pieces. First, readers explore many examples of a particular genre, say, realistic fiction, discovering and discussing criteria for this type of writing. Using these criteria, they co-compose original genre-specific pieces of writing—in this case, a work of realistic fiction.

■ Strategy in Action

Missy's Writers

Missy Taylor's second graders are working on a nonfiction exploration project, the precursor to a nonfiction writing project. Dyads or triads of students are exploring books about "community helpers." Mary, Greg, and Sonya are reading *Nurses* (Ready 1997), a short, nonfiction text in a series called Community Helpers. Their task is to summarize each page of text in three sentences. Each child has a copy of the text. They have chosen to read chorally, but are having trouble getting started.

Greg: Okay, we're not agreeing on this. (*begins reading*)

Missy arrives and reminds them of the T-A-S-K chart (see Figure 1–1 for an example of a T-A-S-K chart) that she used to introduce the writing activity. The three writers hunch together, Mary acting as scribe.

Mary: (*writes*) *Nurses help people who are sick. Nurses check people's blood pressure.*
Sonya: Nurses check people's hearts.
Mary: What did you say?
Sonya: (*repeats her sentences*)
Mary: (*writes*) *Nurses check people's heart.*
Sonya: (*points to* heart) *s.*
Mary: (*adds the* s)

Across the classroom, Mike, Lynn, and Les are engaged in a similar task, except their subject is astronauts. Missy usually specifies that writers take turns acting as scribe, but she has given children the option to decide what works best for them today. These three writers have agreed that Lynn will scribe for this task, and "next time" someone else will have a turn. They are using the text *Astronauts* (Deedrick 1998), also in the Community Helpers series. As Lynn begins writing, Mike and Les talk simultaneously, offering many suggestions.

Lynn	Mike	Les
Hold on! I can't write that fast!		
	There are different types of astronauts.	
[*writes*] *There are different tips of astronauts.*		
		Astronauts have to go to college.

[writes] *Astronauts have to finish collig to learn about space.*

What about the pictures?

They . . . the astronauts have to go into space to take pictures.

[writes] *They have to go into space to take pitchers of the eath. They ex . . .*

Well, let's go to the next page.

They experiment in space?

[nods]

[writes] *They ex [checks the book for spelling] periment space to live there. Astronauts help . . .*

[grabs the paper]

Hey! [takes paper and writes] *us understand the eath [checks book and erases "eath"] earth. [looks at her partners]*

[nods]   [nods]

[completes the sentence]
There, finished. Want to make a picture?

Yeah!

[Draws an astronaut]

Missy's writing partners are practicing their summarizing skills while reading and examining nonfiction writing samples in preparation for writing their own pieces of descriptive writing. In this case, writing has slowed down the reading process, enabling partners to examine the genre closely through discussion and summarizing.

Kristine's Writers

Kristine Kefor's third graders are also involved in an activity linking reading and writing processes. They are actively researching and replicating an aspect of narrative—characterization—in preparation for writing their own stories. First, Kristine gathers the class on the carpet to introduce the partner-writing activity. She reminds students about the previous day's talk on characters and character traits. The story they are using is from their reading series anthology.

Kristine: Today we're going to do some comparing of characters from the story. Does anyone have any ideas about what I mean by "comparing?"

Child 1: To show things in common.

Child 2: To show things they don't have in common.

Kristine: Yes, things in common and things that are different. You can do two or three circles on your paper . . . or even four circles for your Venn diagram.

Kristine: (*reminds them about previous Venn diagram work. Some partnerships completed their Venn comparing/contrasting the previous day.*) Okay, who's ready to write a paragraph?

There follows a short discussion about writing with a partner and appropriate behavior.

Kristine: Who holds the pen?

Child 3: We share.

Kristine: That's right. Each writer needs a chance to hold the pen. How have people been sharing this job?

Child 4: One person writes a paragraph, then we switch and other person writes next one.

Kristine: Yes, did that work for you last time? (*child nods*) So, you'll do it again?

Kristine suggests that writers say their ideas out loud so their partners can hear/add to/help, and so on.

Child 5: What about three partners? (*there are several triads in this class*)

Child 6: Each write a sentence?

Kristine: Or maybe a couple? That way you allow a few more ideas to come out.

She then reminds them to:

- Write with your partner.
- Read with your partner.
- Peer edit with your partner.

Kristine: What can you do when you get stuck?

Children volunteer the following ideas:

- Look at the chart.
- Look in the book [story].
- Look in a dictionary.
- Ask your partner.

Kristine: Who is the last person you should ask?
Several children: The teachers!

Kristine calls students' attention to a blank piece of chart paper and writes down some criteria and rules that the students generate for this work. The children then disperse to collect their Venn diagrams, paper, and writing implements. Sam and Soren are seated cross-legged, side-by-side on the carpeted floor, their Venn diagram in front of them, their writing paper nearest them. Sam is acting as scribe.

Sam	**Soren**
[*writes*] *Thomas and grandfather have many differences. First,* [*adds later, see below "grandfather"*] *favorite cind of animal*	
	[*reads what Sam has written silently, then leans over and adds 's' in cinds—kinds*]
[*writes*] *is a dog.* . . . *and Thomas likes cats.*	
	I want to write Thomas!
Next paragraph is your turn. [*continues writing*] *Thomas is young and short and grandfather is* . . .	
	tall and old
[*writes*] *tall and old.*	

At this point, I query them about how they had decided to share the writing task and they tell me that on their Venn diagram, Soren had written the character traits for Thomas, Sam had written the grandfather's traits, and that they had both added ideas to the middle (traits the characters have in common).

Sam	Soren

Sam

[*stops writing and moves marker to Venn diagram where he crosses out the information he has used in his paragraph*]

What do you think we should do next?

[They have a short discussion.]

Soren

[*underlines information on the Venn diagram that Sam should use for his next sentence*]

[*writes*] Grandfather has very little hair and [*later adds, "but"*] Thomas has a lot of hair.

[Both writers study their Venn diagram.]

Voice? [*meaning should they write about the characters' voices*]

So . . . [*writes*] Grandfather had a voice like a tuba and [*adds later "but"*] Thomas had a voice like a pennywhistle.

What should we write next?

Kristine checks in and suggests that they go back and reread their entire story before they continue. They reread. Sam recognizes that he forgot the word *grandfather* in the second sentence and inserts it. Kristine points to sentence four and wonders aloud whether there is anything they'd like to change. They decide to insert *but* after *hair*. The boys then discuss sentence five and decide to change *and* to *but* to continue the pattern of the previous sentence.

Along with the seven other partnerships at work around the classroom, Sam and Soren continue building their summary of character traits using information from their Venn diagrams and referring back to the story many times to verify information and acquire additional material. When they will later co-compose a story, this focus on characterization continues as Kristine asks them to develop characters with specific traits that they will incorporate into their narrative.

In both classrooms, teachers design tasks that foster active, collaborative research. Partners' research is then applied to a specific writing activity—summarizing—making explicit connections between reading and writing for children that they will later apply to co-composing and independent writing.

There are many similarities between reading and writing processes and making these explicit to writers strengthens all literacy skills. Samway (2006) identifies the following similarities or connections:

- Both reading and writing involve *revision* and fixing up as learners assess meaning in texts read or penned.
- Both reading and writing involve *preparation* in the form of prereading—scanning the text, asking questions, predicting—and prewriting—thinking, researching, asking questions, and organizing.
- Both reading and writing involve constructing meaning.
- Both reading and writing involve what Samway (2006) calls "a public act of sharing" (104) as readers discuss books or share a piece of writing.
- Both reading and writing involve risk taking and errors.
- Both reading and writing are transactional processes whereby the reader or writer brings her experiences, background, and opinions to bear on text read or created.
- Both reading and writing "involve the creation of original text" (Samway 2006, 105). Just as writers create meaning in what they compose, meaning does not flow in an unbroken form from print to reader, but always involves reader intervention in the form of interpretation, responses, and description.

Two Roles When Focusing on Genre

When students explore and study genre, they continually move between reading and writing processes. Writing slows down the reading process for learners and enables them to more carefully analyze language that is read or spoken. Writing also seduces readers into switching between different sources of knowledge and using what they know without formal analysis of language and grammar.

In exploring genre, writing partners might assume one of two roles: (1) genre analyst, where partners read a specific genre, take notes, and organize information in order to jointly compose a reading response based on their analysis of some aspect of text, or (2) genre author, where partners study text in order to extract genre-specific criteria, which they then use to co-compose an example of the genre.

Genre Analyst   The classroom snapshots in this chapter show students acting as genre analysts who draw information from text in order to use it in their reading response. Both snapshots represent structured ways to explore genre and make explicit reading–writing connections for students. In both cases, writing partners examine text in order to extract certain kinds of material before writing a summary. The task for Missy's second-grade partners is to extract the main idea, then summarize. For Kristine's third graders, partners focus on a specific aspect of the narrative—character traits—then extract information from the story, organize it using a Venn diagram, and write a summary that compares and contrasts traits of Thomas and grandfather.

Fourth-grade teacher Cindy Pasieka says, "students need to be able to read informational texts, or any texts, and draw out what's important. Often, they read silently, then simply discuss with a partner. This is really valuable." Both Missy's and Cindy's students study nonfiction texts in order to extract information, organize, then co-compose summaries highlighting main ideas and details.

Genre Author   Toward the end of the year, when her fourth graders are experienced collaborators, Cindy has them partner up to co-compose poems. This joint composing occurs at the conclusion of the class poetry unit; the children have spent weeks studying and reading poems, giving them many models from which to draw as they compose their original poems. Many of the poems have specific, defined structures and conventions. Through their study, children have extrapolated knowledge about structures and conventions, invaluable when they begin to compose their own poems. As "genre authors," they can now monitor and shape their performance. Appendix B contains a blank genre research form that teachers can use.

Darline Berrios' second graders use genre sheets when beginning a study of a specific genre. Throughout the year, they explore examples of realistic fiction, letter writing, persuasive writing, narrative, descriptive writing, and other genres for the purpose of drawing out criteria that they can use as writers. When they begin their reading research, Darline frequently has them work as partners to complete genre sheets (Figure 14–1). Figure 14–2 illustrates another genre sheet used in the midst of a poetry unit, when Diana Lanze's fifth graders take time to examine what they notice about poetry.

After completing their genre research, partners share information with the entire class and everyone identifies the specific structures, conventions, and characteristics of the genre that become the criteria for writers. As a result, writers pay conscious attention to genre criteria when they begin writing their own pieces.

Genre Research Form

Names _Gina_ _Kayla_

Date _12-8_ Title _I Am Thankful for..._

What we notice about _poetry_ ...
(genre under study)

Notes

- there are lot's of lists
- there is vivid language
- the poem goes from a negative to a positive
- there are important reasons to like the bad things

Comments and Criteria

- diffent forms
- musical

FIG. 14–1 *Realistic Fiction Genre Sheet*

Minilessons to Support Partners' Genre Explorations

Literature models are key, no matter what the genre of writing students explore. Prior to beginning a genre study, teachers gather many examples of illustrative or mentor texts, then develop minilessons and plan discussions using these texts. There are a few general suggestions to consider when planning minilessons:

1. Provide space for partners to share what they have discovered in research into genre.
2. Create charts, webs, and diagrams with students, listing genre research information and criteria.

Name: Skylar and Kara   11/21

Title: <u>Ben's tooth</u> Author: <u>Beverly</u>

What we notice about realistic fiction...

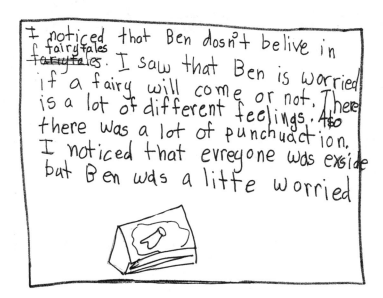

I noticed that Ben dosn't belive in
~~fairytales~~ fairytales. I saw that Ben is worried
if a fairy will come or not. There
is a lot of different feelings. Also
there was a lot of punchuaction.
I noticed that evreyone was exside
but Ben was a litte worried

FIG. 14-2 *Poetry Genre Sheet*

3. Provide time for modeling by authors—teacher, other adults, or students—where they share influences on their writing.
4. Read about professional authors' routines and writing processes.
5. Invite professional authors of a particular genre in to share their craft and answer student questions.
6. Collect "little bits of writing" when reading and sharing with the whole class. Partners typically love to do this, using sticky notes, index cards, or response journals.
7. Use mentor or touchstone texts (Nia 1999). These are texts that writers identify as illustrative of the genre, texts to which they refer again and again while reading and writing in a certain genre.

Reading and writing are social acts. Authors read the writing of others and share thoughts with others. Responses can be verbal or written. Writers compose texts for readers, which others read and respond to. In genre explorations, writing partnerships provide continual modeling, feedback, and discussion for readers and writers as the lines between literate processes are blurred, made explicit, then blurred again.

■ Moving Toward Independence

Once writers have studied a genre with their partner, drawn out essential characteristics and criteria, shared with the whole class, and finally co-composed a genre-specific piece, they have internalized habits and knowledge that will enable them to embark on individual writing assignments with greater confidence and skill.

Certainly, once partners have co-composed a genre-specific piece, the natural extension is to ask them to write their own summary, descriptive piece, narrative, poem, or realistic fiction. These independent-writing pieces can then be shared, first with partners, who act as supportive listeners or editing buddies (see Chapter 10), then shared with the teacher or the entire class. Partners know each other's style and voice, and usually listen with greater insight and expertise, thus aiding each other's development and confidence in ways less-attuned teachers and peers cannot. Teachers can use, or adapt and change, the following suggested sequence to suit their writers and programs:

1. *Partners research texts.* Partners act as Genre Analysts in order to extract information, discover criteria, and summarize findings.
2. *Partners continue studying genre.* Partners establish criteria specific to the genre and share their research with the entire class.
3. *Partners become Genre Authors.* Partners co-compose a genre-specific piece using established criteria.
4. *Individual writers compose genre-specific pieces.* Using criteria established during their roles as analysts, writers create their own examples.
5. *Partners meet to share.* Partners meet and share their individual writing pieces, acting as supportive listeners and editing buddies for one another.
6. *Individual writers revise writing.* After revising, writers share with the whole class or with the teacher.

■ Suggestions for English Language Learners

According to Ovando, Combs, and Collier (2006), "writing stimulates reading. Reading stimulates writing. And talking about one's own writing and other authors' writings, as well as connected experiences leads to cognitive and academic growth through language acquisition: a full circle" (172). This describes perfectly what happens when writing partners explore genre together. In literacy-rich classroom environments, when children collaborate during authentic reading and writing activities, researchers observe them making many connections between these literate processes (Jaggar, Carrara, and Weiss 1986; Lancia 1997): both activities positively influence children's English language acquisition.

When we read aloud to students we provide important literary models for English language learners. When they explore texts with partners, they are

WORDS WE MIGHT FIND IN ....

Title _Sarah morton's Day_____ Date _11-20-06_

Names ___Ruth and Valerie_____

Words we might find are...

WORD	YES	NO
1. Sarah morton	✓	----
2. Pilgrim	----	----
3. Cloths	✓	----
4. school	----	----
5. friends	----	----
6. Chours	✓	----
7. turkey	----	----
8. faimily	✓	----
9. Thanksgiving	----	----
10. Barn	----	----

Comments & Surprises: _____

_____

FIG. 14–3   *"Words We Might Find In ... " Chart*

exposed to many more models, and collaborative contexts, so they can discuss and respond to the literature with peers. The kind of texts we use is important. Mentor or touchstone texts particularly supportive of learning English language learners should contain:

- clear organizational structures
- highly patterned text
- easily discernible style, voice, or tone
- depictions of familiar, real-world concepts, ideas, and situations.

The models we choose should give writing partners a wide variety of opportunities to explore, examine, and "borrow" from important literary works.

In beginning genre study, pay particular attention to students' background and familiarity with genre-specific vocabulary. Bringing vocabulary to the forefront at the prereading, preresearch stage strengthens writers' background knowledge, particularly students learning English. One prereading strategy that writing partners might use to increase vocabulary acquisition is Words We Might Find In . . . (see the blank form in H). Words We Might Find In . . . is adapted from activity described by Nelson and Linek (1999) as Word Wondering and Wandering.

A variation on anticipation guides, this task asks partners to make lists of words they might find in a text before reading. Then, during and after reading, they check "yes" or "no" on their list if they encounter the word. This task takes genre exploration a step further, focusing explicitly on vocabulary and engaging readers and writers in valuable conversations as they predict what the text will hold. The Words We Might Find In . . . activity not only promotes children's active involvement, but also gives learners a preview of vocabulary they might encounter in text, building their background and experience prior to reading (refer back to Figure 14–3).

Research Buddies

It's fun working with a partner. It's like . . . sometimes you get better ideas 'cause you have two minds.

—Fifth grader

CLASSROOM CHALLENGE

How do I help *all* my students, no matter what their ability level or language competency, to confidently approach all phases of research projects and papers?

▨ Research Buddies: What Are They?

Asking students to work alone on challenging, multilayered research projects is far less effective than pairing them with a writing partner to share tasks and thinking. Working collaboratively encourages learners' active participation. Pairs of writers acting as research buddies work together to conduct joint research on a topic—self-selected or teacher assigned—then organize their information and write about it. Depending on curriculum and teacher expectations, research buddies may:

- Select a topic together or be assigned one by their teacher.
- Collect information together through observations, explorations, experiments, and reading.
- Take notes together.
- Co-compose a report outline.
- Co-compose a final summary/report or work independently to compose a final report.

Prior to partners' research work, teachers sometimes demonstrate the process and even write a group report or paper with the whole class in order to model each stage for children. Then partners select a project of their own and begin to work. During this prewriting phase, teachers can pair children informally to gather information or write small segments of text, which they then bring to share with the whole class. This kind of preliminary work ensures that when partners (or individuals) begin, they are clear about process and expectations.

Strategy in Action

Mary Lee's Writers

During the course of the year, my first graders write three "animal reports"— bird, land mammal, and sea creatures. Collaborating is always an option at any stage of this project, and children often choose to work with partners, particularly during the research phase. They seek materials together at libraries, home, and school; amass their resources; read them together; take notes and compare them, and organize their information using a variety of graphic organizers. Usually, students write their own animal report, but occasionally a pair of writers chooses to collaborate right up through the final report, and both writers' names appear on the piece in the class anthology.

I check in with partners, and individual writers frequently during all stages of these report-writing projects. If one person appears to be doing most of the work at any stage, I intervene and make suggestions for how tasks might be shared more equitably. If a child wanted to collaborate on all three report projects, I would probably insist that at least one of the three final reports be written individually. First graders typically enjoy the challenge of these projects. They are proud to have their own individual page in the anthology, and each receives a copy to take home. Publishing is a great motivator, and if children collaborate on the first report, they are usually eager to forge ahead on their own for the next.

Cindy's Writers

For Cindy Pasieka's fourth-grade animal research projects, students choose an animal, read, research, and write about the animal's physical characteristics, habitat, diet, adaptations, and more. Art, math, and science activities also tie into her projects. Collaboration is an option for Cindy's students at any stage in the project, but they write individual reports. Students like to collaborate during the research phases, write independently, then regroup to act as supportive listeners or editing buddies during the revision and publishing stages (see Chapter 10).

■ Suggestions, Ideas, and Minilessons for Research Buddies

Typically, we think of research partners in relation to explorations of factual materials, where students gather resources and write up descriptive or informational reports: however, these kinds of partnerships can also be used to research stories, poems, and other fictional materials. Or, research buddies can observe and write about phenomena they encounter firsthand—in the school building and grounds or on field trips. Research buddies can also explore and write about their own or their classmates' interests, hopes, and dreams. Whenever possible, partners should be given the chance to explore subjects about which they are passionate.

Here are some suggestions—for nonfiction, fiction, and firsthand research that writing partners might undertake and for minilessons that address the needs of each area of study. In reading through the lists, teachers will, no doubt, think of other ideas relevant to their own students and program.

Biography Writing

In writing a biography partners collaborate to write:

- *Buddy Biographies*. Partners interview and study *a peer*, then collaborate to write a biography. This is a great prequel to "real-life" or "famous-person" biography writing. Children can hone their interview skills and learn about chronological order, time lines, and a biographical style of writing, without extensive reading and text-based research.
- *Famous-Person Biographies*. Partners read about and study *a famous person*, then collaborate to write a biography.
- *Real-Life Biographies*. Partners interview and study *an adult they know*, then collaborate to write a biography.

Minilessons can include, but are not limited to, the following:

- conducting first-person interviews
- developing interview questions
- finding resources

- writing in chronological order
- reading other biographies and examining biography authors' style, voice, and organizational formats
- moving from notes, interviews, and planning tools, such as maps or graphic organizers, to final report drafts
- editing and revising

Investigating a Topic in Science or Social Studies

Partners choose a topic, then observe, read, research, take notes, organize information, and write a report. Topics of investigation might include:

- animals
- natural-world phenomena
- events
- geographic locations (homes, neighborhoods, towns, states, countries)

Minilessons include, but are not limited to, the following:

- selecting topics or subjects within a topic area
- observing and collecting data
- taking and organizing notes
- using planning tools such as graphic organizers and semantic maps
- moving from planning tools to drafts of reports
- editing and revising together

Investigating Narrative

Partners examine one or several narrative texts, gathering and organizing information (on a graphic organizer, an outline or a semantic map), then summarize their findings in writing. See Appendix J for examples of narrative research tools. Narrative investigations might focus on:

- *Character traits.* Partners collect evidence about character traits, and describe, list, compare, and contrast, or analyze before writing.
- *Setting.* Using many texts, partners focus their attention on setting and the role this literary element plays in narrative text. Their report might list findings and observations, or it might analyze and describe the importance of setting in the texts studied.
- *Plot.* Partners examine one or several texts, noticing elements of plot—beginning, middle, end, problem, solution, rising action, climax, resolution,

etc.—then report their findings through the use of illustrations, graphic organizers, or descriptive reporting.

- *Text Structures.* Children study many fictional examples, noticing and describing the various text structures. They then illustrate, graph, or write up their findings.

Minilessons include, but are not limited to, the following:

- locating mentor texts
- discovering criteria for narrative writing
- planning for writing using story maps or graphic organizers
- moving from planning tools to draft
- editing and revising together

Firsthand Research

Partners observe, take notes, and report about something they observe firsthand in their world such as:

- weather changes
- what's outside the window
- their home
- the classroom
- their neighborhood
- what they notice on a class field trip

Minilessons include, but are not limited to, the following:

- selecting a topic
- observing and notetaking
- organizing notes and findings
- moving from notes to a first draft
- incorporating photos, graphs, and other visuals
- editing and revising together

Literature models support students' nonfiction writing and help partners zero in on their craft. A useful resource for minilessons that focus on nonfiction writing is Fletcher and Portalupi's (2001) *Nonfiction Craft Lessons: Teaching Informational Writing, K–8.* The minilessons and literature suggestions in this clearly written, user-friendly volume always spark ideas for craft lessons using literature *we love.*

A Word About Text Structure

If we want to encourage diversity and variety in partners' reporting, particularly when they are writing nonfiction, we should provide writers with explicit instruction and frequently expose them to models of different text structures. When I introduce and discuss a text structure—for example, "compare and contrast"—I also create and post a visual reminder, in the form of a chart or illustration, to which partners can refer when writing. Some text structures we may want to highlight for writers include:

- narrative structure
  - beginning, middle, and end
  - plot structure
  - elements of story (characters, setting, etc.)
- chronological order
- compare and contrast
- enumeration
- problem and solution
- question and answer

When modeling text structures, I am careful to emphasize that most texts contain a variety of structures depending on the information to be conveyed. It is delightful to watch children play with these structures—copying authors' style and incorporating a variety of formats that make their writing more interesting (see the description of Betsy's writing in Chapter 18). At least initially, this type of play may be even more fun with a buddy.

A Word About Report Formats

Partner reports can take many forms and often include illustration, charts, graphic organizers, photographs, video clips, and other multimedia. While this book focuses on *writing* partnerships, children of any age can collaborate on writing in many ways. For example, they could use video clips accompanied by a script or video plan. Charts, graphs, illustrations, photographs, and other visuals included in a report can and should be accompanied by detailed captions that reveal the research rationale for including them.

■ Moving Toward Independence

At any stage of research and writing, many teachers allow children to choose whether to collaborate or work alone. In this way, writers move continually between collaboration and independent writing. Here is one approach that teachers might find helpful in implementing a research writing project:

1. The teacher models the process by creating a "group writing piece" with the whole class.
2. Partners research and create a partner-writing piece.
3. Students research and write a piece independently.

No matter how teachers structure projects, research buddies can and do support and assist each other at every stage, providing tools, skills, and confidence that they then carry with them into independent writing and research.

■ Suggestions for English Language Learners

The Units of Study approach (Nia 1999), where reading and writing follow themes and curriculum is integrated across subject areas (such as math, science, art, etc.) supports vocabulary and language acquisition for English language learners. The use of mentor and touchstone texts exposes writers to good literature models again and again in a variety of contexts, demystifying language structure and vocabulary for learners.

When working with a "research buddy," English language learners, like all students, may also benefit from the use of semantic grids (Nelson and Linek 1999; Bromley 1991) to organize and record key vocabulary; examine word attributes, discuss the relationships and relevance of vocabulary to text, and acquire new conceptual understandings (see Appendix J for a blank Web of Information of semantic grid). The analytic frameworks of semantic grids provide a simple, straightforward way for all learners to practice and play with vocabulary, drawing conclusions and engaging in a low-risk, problem-solving activity.

■ Resources

Two resources I use when planning nonfiction writing projects are Tony Stead's (2002) book *Is That a Fact? Teaching Nonfiction Writing, K–3* and McMackin and Siegel's (2002) wonderful book, *Knowing How: Researching and Writing Nonfiction, 3–8*. Stead gives clear, step-by-step guidelines for every stage of writing, especially the prewriting stage, where we show primary students "how." McMackin and Siegel offer teachers many strategies for getting intermediate writers started; for keeping them writing from paragraph to paragraph revising and assessing in order to strengthen leads and conclusions and attend to transitions; and, finally, for showing them how to step back and appreciate their success.

16 Real-Life Collaborations: Writing with Purpose and Specificity

It's fun to meet someone [new] and not actually work alone and always have to be quiet. You actually talk about real stuff.

—Fifth grader

CLASSROOM CHALLENGE

How do I support students' active collaboration and joint problem solving when I recognize these as critical "real-life" skills?

■ Real-Life Collaborations: What Are They?

One could argue that all writing is "real life," and this would be correct, but what distinguishes this strategy is the writers' deliberate focus on a type of real-world writing toward a particular purpose or goal. Just as the name implies, this writing is specifically designed with real-life applications in mind. And, like the strategy of community messages (Chapter 13), "real-life writing" requires partners to carefully consider the audience, or the real-world application.

No matter what the type of real-life writing a teacher selects, this strategy will always involve identifying a specific need, problem, or purpose for writing partners' work. Teachers model asking questions, then encourage partners to develop their own. Teachers also guide students as they retrieve and analyze data and develop guidelines and structures for their final writing pieces.

An example of real-life writing would be co-composing travel brochures—a real-life type of persuasive writing with a specific purpose to entice the reader to visit a place. During the course of the year, Cindy Pasieka's fourth-grade and British educator Emma Smith's third-year writing partners compose travel brochures. After the teachers explain the task and present many sample brochures to the entire class, partners disperse to examine brochures more closely, discussing their unique features and design. They then make observational notes to share with the class. Following a wholeclass sharing of this preliminary research, each writing partnership selects a geographic region or area to research and write about for their brochure.

Partners' research takes them to the Internet: to their school, home, and public libraries: and to their classroom resource collection. For this project, an excellent resource is local travel agencies; owners are often happy to donate brochures and other materials for student projects. After doing the research, partners co-compose alluring descriptions to entice would-be travelers to visit their destination.

Cindy and Emma teach an ocean apart—Emma in southern England, Cindy in New York—yet both have discovered the power of writing collaborations for their eight and nine-year-old writers. These purposeful, real-life writing tasks motivate students, encourage active research, and inspire persuasive and passionate writing about subjects about which children have become "experts."

■ Cindy's Writers

Cindy Pasieka begins her fourth-grade writers workshop by reviewing a familiar writing structure, T-A-S-K (see Chapter 1).

Cindy: What is TASK? How would you explain it to someone from outside our school building?
Student 1: It's for planning your writing.
Cindy: Yes. It is for planning and organizing your writing. We'll be using TASK today to organize our first paragraph in our New York travel brochures.

Cindy leads the discussion into writing persuasively, calling students attention to the persuasive writing chart (see Figure 16–1) and asking them to give examples of persuasiveness. Students take turns telling a short story. After each narrative, Cindy asks the group why each story is convincing. Finally, she says,

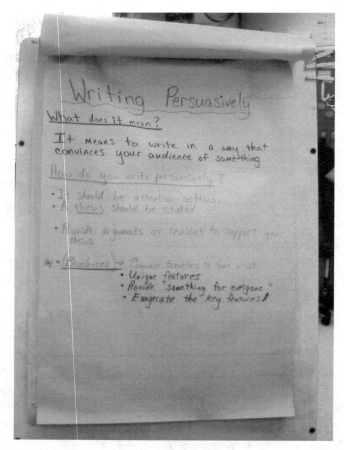

FIG. 16–1   *Cindy's Persuasive Writing Chart*

"When you write persuasively, you are trying to convince someone through your writing. Why do we do this?"

The discussion continues as Cindy uses a sample travel brochure she has written to demonstrate a number of elements such as:

- Identifying a thesis (T).
- Stating details (A) that support the thesis, which in the case of the travel brochures is persuading people to travel to their region of New York.
- Writing brochure copy in a way that argues for reasons to travel to New York (A).
- Writing a summarizing sentence (S) to conclude their brochure paragraph.
- Keeping to the topic (K) and the brochure section students choose to write about first—geography, climate, attractions, or resources.

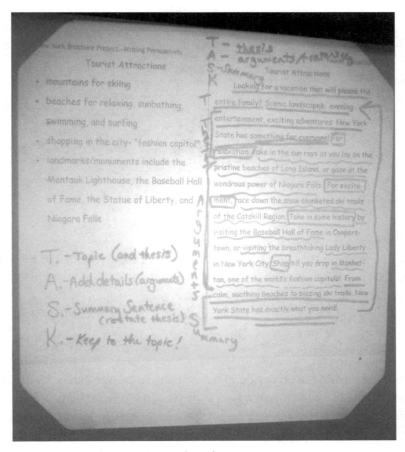

FIG. 16–2 *Cindy's Sample Travel Brochure*

Cindy reads through her writing sample and asks students to identify all elements of T-A-S-K (see Figure 16–2). Writing partners disperse to begin writing their own paragraphs on whichever section of the brochure they have selected. Like Cindy, they will identify and pay attention to T-A-S-K elements as they write.

Janelle and Ellie sit side by side, consulting their notes from the previous day's writing. They have decided to write about "attractions" for their region, northern New York, and they discuss how they will begin and what information from their notes they want to include. They engage in tentative, constructive talk, making suggestions, changing their minds, and moving back and forth from notes to their paragraph draft. Snippets of their talk sound like this:

Janelle: What about . . . ? Like . . . ? (*points to her notes*)
Ellie: In the . . . you can watch . . . ?

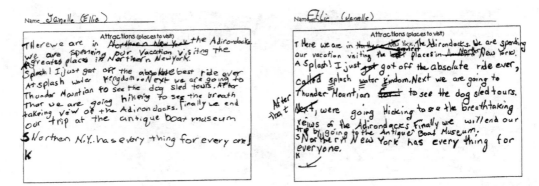

FIG. 16–3 *Buddies' Travel Brochure Paragraph Drafts*

Janelle: (makes an inaudible suggestion)

Ellie: I agree with that, but I think that [Janelle's sentence] should be in the middle, not the beginning.

Janelle: Let's do the topic sentence.

Ellie: (points to her notes) I think we should do [write about] this first, then that. *(points to Janelle's notes)*

They spend several minutes discussing sentence order and where they will include information, then decide to reread their drafts (see Figure 16–3). They plan together, but each is writing her own version of the draft. As they reread, they continually revise and edit spending the bulk of their time orally planning what they will say and how to say it before writing. Their completed paragraph reads as follows:

> Here we are in the Adirondacks. We are spending our vacation visiting the greatest places in northern New York. Splash! I just got off the absolute, best ride ever at Splash Water Kingdom. Next we are going to Thunder Mountain to see the dog sled tours. After that, we're going hiking to see the breathtaking views of the Adirondacks. Finally, we end our trip by going to the Antique Boat Museum. Northern New York has everything for everyone!

Writing activities like this one, composing travel brochures, involve students in authentic writing projects that make specific connections to real-world issues, problems, activities, or, in this case, real geographic regions. Janelle and Ellie's talk reveals their active collaboration and continual problem solving as they co-compose their persuasive piece. As they work to convince people to travel to northern New York, they are developing important, real-life skills that extend beyond this project.

■ Steps and Procedures

Creating travel brochures "is an ideal project for partners," Emma says, "because the more able students seem to think more about their writing and what they're doing when they work with others, particularly when they're helping others. On their own, more able students tend to rush to complete writing pieces, but when they work in partnership, they slow down and are more thoughtful . . . the quality of their writing really improves." This slowing-down happens whenever writing partners work together. Collaboration may not always be as "efficient" as independent writing, but the benefits to writers are longer-lasting.

Real-life writing projects, whether designed for partners or individual writers, take many directions and pathways, but always begin with questions before immersing writers in the genre where they will study examples, identify touchstone or mentor texts, establish criteria and conduct research for their writing, and finally, compose a text that contributes new voices to the issue at hand. Stages and activities for a real-life writing project would most likely include the following:

- Identify a need, problem, or purpose.
- Study the genre form that best suits the writers' purpose.
- Establish criteria for writing.
- Research the topic.

- Organize all information, "putting pieces together."
- Compose final reports.

At each stage of writing, teachers should offer minilessons designed to introduce next steps, clarify expectations, and provide time for students to share and discuss challenges and successes.

Identifying a Need, Problem, or Purpose

When asking partners to research and write about a real-life topic, need or problem, teachers must identify a particular genre to accomplish their purpose. For Cindy and Emma's travel brochures project, the genre is persuasive writing. Minilessons at this stage may focus on:

- brainstorming and sharing what students know about the type of writing (in this case travel brochures)
- immersing partners in the reading of sample or mentor texts
- leading students in generating "big questions" about their topic
- continuing to encourage partners' further questions as they plunge into active research

Studying the Genre Form and Establishing Criteria for Writing

At this stage, using Cindy and Emma's projects as an example, partners study actual travel brochures, travel advertisements, and Internet sites. They gather travel materials from their parents, relatives, and local travel agencies. Finally, they scour websites devoted to travel. As partners study these texts, they discuss the characteristics of travel brochures and take notes to share with the class. Minilessons at this stage may focus on:

- identifying and examining mentor or touchstone texts
- establishing criteria for genre writing piece (in this case, a travel brochure that entices the reader to travel to a certain destination) through whole-class discussion

A successful travel brochure might include some of the following:

- interesting visuals (photos of colorful scenery)
- exciting language that invites and entices the reader
- short, colorful descriptions that *show*, don't *tell* about the location
- strong nouns and verbs

Researching the Topic

At this point partners would choose a specific destination, then begin research on their locale. Minilessons at this stage may focus on:

- finding resources and information
- note taking
- identifying "what's important" in sources consulted
- evaluating source materials for accuracy, bias, and relevancy
- using both primary- and secondary-source materials

Primary source materials about travel might include:

- interviews with people—parents, friends, teachers, or community members—who have traveled to their destination
- books, articles, or first-person descriptions of travel to the desired destination

Secondary source materials about travel might include:

- Internet sites
- books
- encyclopedias
- magazine articles
- newspaper travel sections
- travel brochures

Even novels and stories about a particular locale might yield valuable information and colorful descriptions that brochure writers can use.

Composing Final Reports

Once partners complete their research, they begin writing, keeping established partnerships criteria in mind. Minilessons at this stage may focus on:

- *Sharing the pen.* Each writer acts as scribe.
- *Establishing routines and procedures.* Partners should establish routines and procedures for sharing resource gathering, deciding who will seek materials during the writers' workshop and at other times.

■ Suggestions for Real-Life Writing Projects

The possibilities for real-life writing projects are many and varied. The types of resources needed will depend entirely on the project undertaken. Real-life writing projects take many forms. While travel brochures are created to inform, persuade, and describe, an editorial about a global issue may be strictly informative; or an advertisement deliberately descriptive.

Teachers should choose projects that fit the needs of their students and programs, and whenever possible, allow partners to choose a topic they are interested in or passionate about. A few real-life writing project suggestions are:

- researching a global issue and writing an action plan based on research
- researching a local issue and writing an action plan based on research
- writing an opinion piece for the school or local newspaper
- writing a position paper on a topic of concern such as:
  - What age should someone be allowed to apply for a library card?
  - Should there be zoos?
  - Should students have homework? How much?
  - Should the driving age be raised?
  - What kind of pet is best?
  - What is the best program on television?
  - Should a woman be president?
  - What is the healthiest diet for kids?
- Writing how-to pieces for specific audiences
  - how to ride a bike
  - how to play a sport
  - how to bake a cake
- Writing an answer to specific questions
  - Where do hurricanes come from?
  - Why is thunder so loud?
  - How are rainbows made?
  - Why do we need schools?
  - What kinds of training do you need to be a good teacher?

Possible real-life topics could easily fill this entire book. A good source for thinking about real-life, nonfiction writing is Tony Stead's (2002) book *Is That a Fact?* Stead provides structures and procedures for helping students develop nonfiction writing skills. While his book is geared for teachers of primary-grade writers, his lists of nonfiction topics are often appropriate for K through 5 writers.

■ Moving Toward Independence

A natural extension of real-life partner writing for students would be to craft their own "real-life writing piece." Providing time and supportive structures for writers to internalize writing expectations through talk and problem solving with their peers ensures that they will approach independent writing assignments with greater confidence and a much larger skills repertoire.

■ Considerations for English Language Learners

As previously described, discussion and modeling are especially important for students learning English. Real-life writing projects provide further opportunities for modeling, accompanied by discussion and examination of materials and writing examples. These activities also immerse English language learners in elements of culture, helping them to internalize written and oral discourse patterns, to use and practice new vocabulary, and to adapt and interact appropriately in what may be new and heretofore unfamiliar social contexts.

In structuring a real-life collaborative writing activity, teachers should provide clear guidelines and purposes at every stage, reiterating, reinforcing, and reteaching procedures when partnerships or individuals are uncertain. Whenever possible, children should be encouraged to seek out and share materials and examples in their first language. In the case of travel brochures, students may also have valuable resources to share with peers researching a destination in their native country.

Frequent exposure to English vocabulary is critical to ELL students. One vocabulary-building activity for ELLs is to create an "Alpha Listing" (Nelson and Linek 1999) about their topic to share and use as a reference when they write and research. Alpha listings are lists of English vocabulary words that students generate while writing. These words are listed in alphabetical order and used for spelling games such as Concentration or bingo and for writing activities. The list can include the same terms in the students' first language. Lists may also be accompanied by visuals—either student drawings or pictures cut from magazines, catalogues, newspapers, and other sources.

17 | Co-Composing Stories

You don't have to do all the work yourself . . . you have another personality [who] you're working with . . . someone to add ideas and maybe someone you don't know as much.

—Fifth grader

CLASSROOM CHALLENGE

Help! My students' stories are all over the place, the structure and organization unwieldy. How can I help them focus in on narrative structure for their own narrative writing, and, quite frankly, prepare them for the state testing where the prompt often asks for narrative?

■ Co-Composing Stories with a Partner: What Does Co-Composing Look Like?

As is obvious, co-composing stories involves writing fictional narratives. Before sending students off to independently craft original stories, a more supportive sequence begins with direct instruction in story structures and conventions followed by time for students to practice, discuss, problem solve, and co-compose their first original story. Collaborators decide on the ideas they will use and how they will share the pen, then plan, organize, write, and revise stories. Writers of any age, especially younger ones, often plan and begin their stories with illustrations. As they draw and discuss ideas, an illustration may suggest a character or setting that spurs them to write. These activities "promote social cohesion, as well as provide mutual entertainment" (Dyson 1993, 60). Drawing is a joyful activity and often nudges young writers into story writing with laughter and greater confidence.

■ Strategy in Action: Notes from the Field

"There's no more free writing . . . not in today's world. My students are mostly engaged in structured, topic-specific writing [or they are] writing to prompts." (Cindy Pasieka, fourth-grade teacher). Cindy's words are echoed by K through 5 teachers in every school I visit. There is no time in the crowded school schedules of today for free writing beyond opportunities afforded by students' brief journal entries. Even journal writing is frequently prescribed or assigned as a response to literature or to a specific prompt or suggestion. Yet listen to fourth grader Helen speak about story writing with her buddy.

> They [my writing partners] fill in the blanks . . . and remind me to put the beginning and end. She [my partner] helps me a lot. We practiced for ELA [English Language Arts, New York State Writing Assessment] together. You [write] are alone on ELA, but this year I listened when I had to write and I heard my partner's voice. It helped me a lot!

Helen not only sees the value of a collaborative relationship, but also makes connections between free-writing activities and the high-stakes testing that is such a presence in today's school life for writers in grades K through 12. If students are not taking a test, they are preparing—even several grade levels away. Recently, second-grade teachers in a Massachusetts classroom were asked to quiz students using sample questions from the *fourth grade MCAS test* pertaining to poetry and an author's use of metaphoric language. Not only were both the task and concepts tested of questionable relevance to fourth graders, they were totally inappropriate for children two years younger. Unfortunately, this is too often the lot of students and teachers in the test-driven climate created by the No Child Left Behind Act. If students like Helen can be comforted and supported through the stress of high-stakes testing by the lessons and strategies learned in writing collaborations, then that alone may be the strongest rationale for including them in the curriculum.

Test preparation aside, upper-elementary-grade teachers with whom I speak, typically find helping students with story writing to be particularly challenging. Lack of structure in the ramblings of many student stories makes revision difficult. Writers cannot seem to grab hold of their stories; their discombobulated dialogue stretches on for pages. In such narratives, plot and meaning are all but lost, as reader *and* writer struggle to discern who is speaking and why.

There are structures and organizing frameworks we can and do share with writers—a few of which are offered in this chapter—but taming the narrative beast is still somewhat daunting for the solo writer. Having a "curricular conversation [with a buddy] over a common purpose or set of purposes [can help both writers proceed] in a mutually accepted direction" (Applebee 1996, 52) with greater clarity and an overall understanding of the task and tale. As Jamiel, a third grader, told me about writing fiction with his buddy, "When two of us are watching the story, it comes out better."

Usually, If the task and expectations are clear, children will appreciate the opportunity to work with buddies to shape and build stories. They generally begin by discussing plot and characters, deciding where their story will be set, and what voices they will use for story and characters. Writers value these cooperative relationships, which strengthen their independent writing skills, whether writing for a class assignment or completing state assessments.

■ Getting Started and Supporting Partners' Story Writing

Supporting partners' story writing has many aspects and takes many forms, but this discussion centers on process, organization, and literature models. Fortunately, many writing experts—teachers and researchers—have published excellent resources on a wide range of aspects to inspire and teach teachers of writing. A recent favorite of mine is Shelley Harwayne's (2001) *Writing Through Childhood: Rethinking Process and Product.* For years, I have turned to Shelley whenever I need inspiration or I want to remember why I continue to teach after thirty-four years.

Focus on Process

As with all the strategies in this book, story writing with partners begins with attention to how writers will share the task. Some questions teachers should ask themselves before setting guidelines for students are:

- When does collaboration begin?
    - Should partners be seated beside each other during whole-class minilessons while the teacher reads aloud literary models or mentor texts?
    - Should partners plan and write each draft together or separately?
    - What about revision? How will partners handle this stage of writing?
- How will they share the pen?
- Should each partner keep her own copy of the story, or are they producing one shared piece?
- Where will writers find resources?
- What behaviors should be stressed about working together?
    - When a partner is listening, what is his job?
    - Who will seek resources and tools when the writer needs them?

After many years of observing reading and writing partnerships, I am still amazed at the structures and routines that children of all ages develop in collaboration. These ideas do not originate with their teacher; they are uniquely the children's. In fact, in many cases, teachers—myself included—can be unaware of these effective process structures unless we watch closely and regularly invite students to share. Teachers are, therefore, encouraged to make time for partners to share *how* they are sharing the pen and *what* their writing process is with the entire class so everyone can benefit from the collective wisdom and expertise.

Focus on Organization

Even when two authors are paying attention, their stories can derail, like runaway trains shooting off into the countryside, substance falling by the wayside in a cloud of dust. Since most of us do not write like Jon Scieszka, the skilled author of such fractured fairy tales as *The True Story of the Three Little Pigs* (1989), attention to the narrative form in the planning and writing stages aids partners in keeping hold of their stories. Minilessons on organization can involve literary elements such as plot, characters, setting, and tone; or can introduce supportive graphic organizers.

Graphic organizers and story maps are particularly helpful in the prewriting stages. Organizers can be webs or simple outlines. One of the simplest organizers I know is the Go Chart. This and other narrative organizers can be found in Appendix J. Teachers must model and show children how to use any organizers they make available before asking writers to incorporate them into their story-writing work. It is helpful for writers to use these visual organizers with a story that they read or is read to them *before* using these tools to plan their own writing. Minilessons that focus on graphic or visual organizers with writing partners might entail the following steps:

- The teacher introduces a visual organizer, suggesting how partners might use it
- The teacher reads a story aloud.
- The teacher and students complete the visual organizer together.
- The teacher demonstrates and shows how she has used the organizer to write her own story, and the students make suggestions, offer comments, and ask questions.
- Writing partners try using the visual organizer to plot their story and debrief.
- Writing partners share their completed visual organizer whole class.
- Writing partners use the organizer to draft their story.

- Writing partners share their stories whole class and describe how the organizer has aided or supported their writing.

Remember that maps, charts, graphic organizers, and other visual planning aids are *prewriting tools*. They are not the writing, nor should they be the primary focus for long. Just as some adult writers like use outlines, and others would never dream of using such a tool, children have different preferences. Teachers are, therefore, encouraged to listen and respect *what children tell us works for them*, and to provide time and space for them to share these ideas with others. I have observed writing partners effectively using some of the following organizational tools, none of which I, or their teachers, had suggested to them:

- cartoons and sketches
- toys and other props they have gathered from around the classroom or brought from home
- math manipulatives (teddy bear counters, chips, dice)
- blocks (for each "event" in the story)
- rulers (for time lines)
- their fingers (to model and act out character voices and dialogue)
- leaves, sticks, and twigs from the playground (to act as characters, evoke setting, and define action)
- maps (to plot action and develop setting)

All writers need some kind of organizational framework, whether it exists in their head or as a tangible entity. Focusing writers on organization helps them develop their own strategies for story writing. Many times, strategies evolve in partnership and are refined by individuals working on independent pieces. Whether penning their own stories or writing to a prompt on state writing assessments, writers carry strengths from partner work to their solo efforts.

Minilessons Using Literature Models

Teachers read aloud books they love, sometimes many times. Through literature, teachers model examples of story writing, highlighting author styles, devices, and ideas that classroom writers might use in their original stories. Although I often use novels and chapter books to discuss literary elements with writers, picture books are the best self-contained models for minilessons that focus on plot, character, setting, and tone. No matter what the grade level, picture books with strong plots; rich, evocative settings; and vivid characters make wonderful models for story writing.

The books I describe here are just a few of my favorite minilesson standbys. Like all teachers, I am continually discovering new standbys to share with writers. I would not necessarily expect teachers to adopt the stories that I find magical, but to use the stories they love with young writers.

- *Hetty and Harriet* (Oakley 1981) is a wonderful model for plot and the circular style of many stories. It is also a great model for ironic voice, echoed beautifully in Oakley's humorous, detailed illustrations. This is a well-plotted tale by the author of the Church Mouse series, beloved by readers of all ages. Like all his stories, Oakley's plot meanders at first, but is soon racing toward a feverish, exciting climax that carries the reader along on a breathless ride. In *Hetty and Harriet*, two chickens break out of the farmyard and head for the open road, wandering into what, at first glance, seems to be a modern, cozy place but turns out to be a chicken factory where the sun never sets and chickens are expected to produce many eggs or be sent to the dreadful "Fowlfare Factory: Makers of Quality Chicken Pies and Soup." Brave Harriet saves the day, rescuing the hapless Hetty as well as a large contingent of fellow fowl and, after a journey downriver, they arrive back at the barnyard, a just-right place after all. This amusing, circular tale makes a great model for plot, rising action, and character. Oakley's illustrations and accompanying text beautifully juxtapose settings—the bucolic, peaceful farm and the dreary, dark, smoke-filled Fowlfare. Another favorite is Oakley's *Church Mice at Bay* (1978), a tale featuring an hilarious plot and wonderfully delineated characters. Truth be told, it especially delights children because—like dePaola's *Bill and Pete* (1978)—at one point in the story, the villainous character is caught naked, a sidesplitting plot twist that children love.

- *Fritz and the Beautiful Horses* (Brett 1981) is another model for strong plot featuring heroic, come-from-behind characters and a very satisfying resolution. I love all Jan Brett's beautiful books for children, but the tale of Fritz, the heroic, sturdy, dependable pony, has always been one of my favorites. This plot-driven story has a clear beginning, middle, and end, the rising action giving way to an exciting, satisfying climax and conclusion. Characters are clearly delineated—the elegant, vain, and beautiful horses whom the ladies and gentlemen of the kingdom ride, as do their children, who look frightened atop the proud steeds; and the short-legged, scruffy pony Fritz, who, despite his prancing and attempts to take "long, graceful strides," is ignored, ridiculed, and rejected by all. When a bridge cracks, the kingdom's children are stranded on one side, adults on the other. The children's proud horses refuse to ford the river, and it is strong, brave Fritz who comes to their rescue, carrying each child to safety. The ending finds Fritz enjoying a "special place in the kingdom," well-loved by all.

- *How Droofus the Dragon Lost His Head* (Peet 1971). The plot has a clear beginning, middle, and end and an exciting climax, followed by one of Peet's signature humorous resolutions. If writing partners are planning tales with brave knights and mythical kingdoms, Peet's loping, loopy tale is the lighthearted story to share with them. As may be apparent, "heroic fiction" and humor are favorites of mine, and the tale of Droofus, the little dragon who loses his way and ends up alone in a dark cave, is a fine example of heroic fiction filled with danger, hardships, touching moments, and a hero with a heart of gold who saves a farmer and his family from famine and then is rescued from beheading by his friend, the clever farm boy, who devises a solution that satisfies a king. Characters are well drawn and they develop and grow as the story progresses.

- *Dogger* (Hughes 1988). Another plot-driven story, this is a tale of loss and the power of familial love, providing writers with examples of the quiet heroism possible in everyday life, with ordinary people like themselves. British author Shirley Hughes is a wonderful writer; her warmhearted stories of young children's experiences perfectly complemented by her soft, realistic illustrations. And *Dogger*—titled *David and Dog* in the United States—is my favorite Hughes book. This is a story about loss—in this case, David's beloved stuffed dog—and redemption, a story of an almost disastrous twist of fate, and a story of sibling love and kindness in the face of adversity. All of this over the loss and recovery of a stuffed animal! Young children (ages three to eight) love this story, and its plot is clear and recognizable to writers. The beginning focuses on family life and the loss of Dogger, then the middle switches to the crowds and lively events of the community "jumble sale," where Dogger is located but inaccessible and sold to another child at the "Toy Stand" just as David spots him. Finally, there is the ending when Dogger, through the kindness of David's sister, Bella, is returned to his rightful owner. A wonderful model for writers!

- *The Lotus Seed* (Garland 1993). This is an exquisite, quietly told story with soft, lovely illustrations by Tatsuro Kiuchi. The plot is clear and the characters speak through their actions in this evocative tale about a Vietnamese grandmother who arrives in a strange country with nothing remaining from her beloved homeland except one tiny lotus seed, which reminds her of the day she saw her emperor cry. Grandmother keeps her precious seed in a secret place until her grandson takes it away to plant. It is a story of loss and the terrible pain of one more thing taken away, as the grandmother mourns the loss of her seed, the symbolic remnant of a faraway past. It is also, finally, a tale of love and redemption, and of one generation passing on to the next as a lotus flower blossoms in the spring and her grandchildren each take a seed to keep in a secret place for the future.

- *Strega Nona* (dePaola 1975). The humor in this now classic story, along with the engaging characterizations and elements of fairy tales and folktales provide many ideas for writing buddies as they build a similar story. There is a clear beginning and middle, with a wryly apt conclusion. The tale of Strega Nona, "Grandma Witch" and her magic pasta pot evokes memories of other tales such as "The Pot That Would Not Stop Boiling" (Rojankovsky 1944) where curiosity and disobedience land the main character, Big Anthony, in a heap of trouble. Big Anthony's troubles begin when he uses the magic pasta pot against the expressed wishes of his employer, Strega Nona. Soon, pasta is burbling and bubbling into the town of Calabria, threatening to engulf the citizenry. The ending finds Big Anthony a little heftier than before, since his punishment is to eat all the pasta before sundown.
- *The Araboolies of Liberty Street* (Swope 1989). A great model for character, change, and comeuppance, this is a joy to read and fun to emulate. Writers of all ages delight in the antics of the colorful Araboolies, who move into a dull, lifeless neighborhood and really shake things up. The story's opening introduces us to the dreary place called Liberty Street where houses all look the same; the children stay indoors, forbidden to play; and fat General Pinch, and his skinny wife preside, threatening to call out the army if anyone disobeys them. The irrepressible Araboolies are oblivious to the rules and edicts of General and Mrs. Pinch, and their lifestyle begins to rub off on the denizens of Liberty Street, finally resulting in the abrupt and unexpected departure of the Pinches in a humorous and delightful twist of fate. Like Pinkwater's *Big Orange Splot* (1977), this amusing tale has much to offer developing writers. The dialogue is sparse, but right on target, sharply defining the "villains" of the story, the dreaded Pinches. Barry Root's illustrations capture the Araboolie's colorful approach to life perfectly.
- *The Mitten* (Brett 1989). A great example of rising action and a climax with a real bang! There are many versions of this folktale. As a model for young writers, I like Jan Brett's because—as in most of her books—her illustrations foreshadow what will come next, giving children another device to use in their writing. As the animals crowd into the mitten for shelter, the story builds to its inevitable climax when a brown bear squeezes in, sneezes and the mitten bursts, sending all occupants flying.
- *The Legend of the Bluebonnet* (dePaola 1983). Many children have this kind of quiet story to tell and this model gives them many tools to get them started.

This beautiful Comanche legend is a tale of hardship, community, and a child's sacrifice for the good of her tribe. I love the quiet tone of this story, the lilting language, and understated resignation of She-Who-Is-Alone as she carefully makes the decision to sacrifice her most prized possession, her warrior doll, to the fires lit to beseech the Great Spirit for rain.

- *The Raft* (LaMarche 2000). Some children want to tell stories like their own lives, only fiction. This lovely tale of a boy and his grandmother evokes a strong sense of place and is a great model for a minilesson on setting. There is also a slowly building relationship between characters that provides writers with insights into how characters change and grow in response to what life, or plot twists, brings them. Best for older writers, grades three to five, but a wonderful read-aloud for any age.

I always delight when I hear the words or expressions from a favorite text aped or paraphrased in a young writer's work. As they build their collective voice and style, writers pore over model texts, selecting the structures, tone, and vocabulary that make their own stories come alive. This list represents just some of my favorites. See Appendix C for a listing of additional literature titles to use as models for plot, character, setting, and tone.

Friends, colleagues, and children are always introducing me to new books that can serve as models for writing buddies and individuals. If we are to use literature in this way, it is critical that writers have opportunities to read and reread these stories. Teachers read-aloud mentor or touchstone texts many times. Beyond the read-aloud time, however, children need access to these models when writing. If books are beyond their reading level, having them on tape and available in a listening center is advisable. Older students or adult volunteers can also be recruited to provide multiple readings.

■ Variations on a Theme

Many teachers, myself included, share multiple versions of a classic tale such as "Cinderella" or the "Three Little Pigs" or explore variations on a theme such as boy-and-dog stories or tales of witches and kings. We live in an age when the children's literature is widely available and easily accessible through inter-library loans so we can decide to do a Cinderella Unit, and put out a call to our local librarian who will collect dozens of versions of this universal tale from many cultures and traditions. One of my favorite Cinderella versions is *Sidney Rella and the Glass Sneaker* (Myers 1985), a come-from-behind football story!

Title	Hero / Heroine	Tormentors / Villains	Kindly "Magical" Helper?	Magical Objects	Significant "Other" Item / Goal
Cinderella (Bros. Grimm)	Cinderella	Stepmother Stepsisters	fairy godmother	glass slipper	Prince
Oochigeaskw Rough Skin (Algonquin legend)	Oochigeaskw Rough Skin	Sisters	~	~	Invisible One
Sidney Rella & the Glass Sneaker	Sidney Rella	brothers	fairy "godfather"	glass sneaker	~
Angkat: Cambodian Cinderella	Angkat	Stepmother / Step-sister	Magical fish Spirit-of-Nature	golden slippers	Prince
Dinorella: A Prehistoric tale	Dinorella	Dora & Doris	Fairydactyl	diamond	Duke Dudley
Cap o' Rushes	Cap o' Rushes	father	~	ring in the gruel	Master's son
Cinderella Penguin or, The Little Glass Flipper	Cinderella	Stepmother & Stepsisters	Great Fairy Penguin	glass flipper	Prince

FIG. 17–1 *Cinderella Variations: Compare and Contrast Chart*

When I undertake a thematic literature unit with children, we keep a chart of familiar story elements as stories are read aloud (see Figure 17–1). This chart becomes a road map when incorporating conventions and structures in a whole-class variation on the theme.

If at some point during the unit, writing buddies or individuals decide to pen their own variation on the theme, a supportive sequence might be as follows:

- The teacher reads aloud many texts fitting the theme.
- The teacher discusses each variation with students.
- Teacher and students chart familiar elements, structures, and conventions.
- Teacher and students complete the story as a shared or guided writing activity, telling a variation on the theme.
- Writing partners collaborate on a joint story following the theme.
- Individual writers compose their own variation on the theme (I usually leave this as an option for writers which they may select at any point for the rest of the school year).

■ Moving Toward Independence

The thematic unit progression helps writers take the skills and strategies learned in partnership to craft their own stories. All the activities and suggestions outlined in this chapter, strengthen individuals' skills and confidence and support their solo performances. As teachers nudge writers toward independence, they remind them of the tools and structures learned during direct instruction, guided practice, and partner writing.

◼ Suggestions for English Language Learners

Narrative, with its twists and turns of plot, metaphoric language, and unfamiliar conventions, can be particularly challenging for ELLs. Story writing is an ideal place to occasionally encourage cross-code writing if students are fluent readers and writers in their first language. These stories can be read to partners and the class then translated. They may also provide less daunting ways for English language learners to play with this genre. Two other ideas are outlined here:

1. *Repeated reading and discussion.* Though teachers read and reread stories aloud to all students, they may want to find time for additional reading and discussion of mentor or touchstone texts for children learning English. This is an ideal activity for classroom volunteers—if teachers provide guidelines and expectations for these helpers.
2. *Structured story models.* The complexity of narrative sometimes overwhelms students, particularly those learning English. When beginning a unit on story writing, teachers might try using structured, highly patterned stories as models for writers. There are hundreds of such texts available. Three of my favorites are:
    *   *Someday* (Zolotow 1965). Children love to write "Someday stories" after hearing this highly patterned, imaginative text read aloud. In addition to beginning each page with "someday," Zolotow includes dialogue on every page, providing helpful modeling of this important narrative element
    *   *Suddenly* (McNaughton 1994). Colin McNaughton has written several picture books with simple plots and a repetitive, predictable style. Each page in this tale of Preston the pig, unknowingly pursued throughout the story by a large wolf, ends with "when suddenly," setting the reader up for the action that follows. Children enjoy writing "suddenly stories" or choosing an alternate word to repeat throughout their story.
    *   *Imagine* (Lester 1989). Who doesn't love to imagine themselves on a jungle safari or exploring the open sea from the safety of their own home. This book, enhanced by Lester's detailed, colorful illustrations, leads to many "imagine stories," a great warm-up activity before beginning to shape a fully plotted story.

Writing Like the Author: Exploring Writers' Voice and Style

18

Me and my partner write like Avi. It's really cool.

—Third grader

■ Writing Like the Author: What Is It?

In writing like the author, writing buddies read and explore an author's writing style—such as Shel Silverstein's poetic style—or voice—as in the distinctive voice of Dr. Seuss—for the specific purpose of emulating that author's style or voice in a jointly composed piece. This exploration might begin as a whole-class activity over a few days or a few weeks where the teacher reads aloud one or many texts by the author, then leads focused discussions about an author's style or voice. Partners examine these mentor texts, discussing what they noticed about the writer's style or voice. Following this exploration, partners come back to the whole group, sharing their findings and observations. During such sharing, teachers may list the findings and make them available as a resource, either on chart paper or as individual copies. Partners use this group wisdom about style or voice to co-compose a piece that incorporates the elements of the particular author's style or voice.

■ Strategy in Action

Cheryl Feeney gathers her second graders on the carpet to complete a read-aloud story by Angela Johnson about the Underground Railroad. Cheryl moves the group into writing by reminding them of their work from the previous day and their author study chart about Angela Johnson's books, with their rich and evocative descriptive style, are often written as personal narratives. As historical works, they are part of the second-grade social studies curriculum, but Cheryl also uses Johnson's style and voice as models for children's personal narrative. As she leads students in a brief minilesson, she reminds them of Johnson's style and focuses on partners' roles as Writing Teachers.

First, Cheryl recounts an "amazing incident from yesterday's writers' workshop." Two students, Tim and Amy, were working together. Tim helped Amy write her story, reminding her of the author chart they had created based on Angela Johnson's style and common elements from her narratives. Cheryl then asks the entire class "What happens when writers work together?"

Child 1: They do what you said . . . they don't disturb the teacher.
Child 2: They remind each other of important stuff . . . like the chart [author study chart].
Cheryl: Yes! I think you're ready to become writing teachers. Who's ready? Children: (*raise their hands*)

Cheryl brings out a chart where she has written her own story. Her story reads as follows: "Once when visiting my cousins we went sledding. We had hot chocolate. We went up and down the hill all night long. One time we slid across the ice on the pond. Then we came home."

Cheryl: Could Mrs. Feeney have written more?
Child 3: You could say, "How did you feel?"
Child 4: You could say, "What about the hot chocolate?"
Child 5: You could say, "What about the hill?"
Cheryl: Yes, you could.

She explains that buddies can help each other find the most important part of their story and tell more.

Cheryl: Which do you think is the most important part of my story?

Child 6: I think it's when you said, "slid across the pond."

Cheryl reminds them that only the writer can tell what's the most important part, but that it is helpful to hear what others think and what parts of the story they identify as important or interesting because we are usually writing for an audience. She says, "Remember, the writer owns the story. When I write, I am making a movie in my mind."

Cheryl then describes an accident that happened to her while sledding with her brother, then acts out how she looked and acted with her brother. She reminds them of their roles as writing teachers, then asks, "Anyone have a comment?

Child 7: You could add that part.

Cheryl: Yes. Anything else?

Child 8: That part was exciting. It gave me a picture in my mind.

Cheryl: Hmm . . . I wonder if I'm just starting to find my voice in this story?

Several children nod and a little discussion follows before Cheryl transitions the group into partner writing, reminding them of the rules for partner writing (see Figure 18–1).

As the group disperses, Cheryl tells me, "I'm always working on all of this. Yesterday, I grabbed Ezra Jack Keats' *Snowy Day* for Larry because I saw something in his writing and I said, 'This sounds like Ezra Jack Keats. Let me show you what he did!' So we got the book and we read and I said, 'Where in what I just read to you do you see something you use and something you can use in your writing?' And he could see it in *The Snowy Day*."

■ Getting Started and Supporting Explorations of Style and Voice

This strategy is fun and tremendously supportive of the literate development of all age writers. Kindergartners love to imitate the rolling, rollicking *Chicka Chicka Boom Boom* (Martin and Archambault 1989) through pictures and words. The humorous writing of Jon Scieszka and many others has inspired countless fractured fairy tales penned by young writers working alone or in partnership. Likewise the work of Shel Silverstein and Dr. Seuss has inspired several generations of young poets. When we explore and study authors' style and voice, we unlock literacy mysteries and discover small nuggets of understanding "how it's done."

FIG. 18–1 *Cheryl's Partner Rules Chart*

Voice is an especially elusive quality and, for writers of all ages, developing it is a lifelong journey. I am always surprised when editors and peer reviewers speak of my voice, telling me they can always recognize my contribution in a collaborative piece of writing. What are they hearing and seeing? I ask myself. I write like everyone else, don't I? The answer is no, we all have our own unique voice or perhaps a closet full of voices that we pull out for different types of writing. Rather than asking writers about their own voice, providing them with opportunities to explore and discuss this quality in the work of a favorite author can often be much more effective.

Explorations of style and voice are ongoing in most classrooms as teachers read aloud and discuss literature with children. Two helpful resources for framing these discussions are *Strategies That Work* (Harvey and Goudvis 2000) and *Mosaic of Thought* (Keene and Zimmerman 1997). Through whole-class, guided reading discussions, teachers show students how to explore literature in small groups or pairs: how to make notes, graph ideas, and share their findings with the whole group.

When teaching first grade, I always begin the year by reading *Charlotte's Web* (White 1952) aloud. As the year progresses, I use passages from this book to talk about style, particularly White's deliberate playing with sentence length, list form, and punctuation. Open an E. B. White novel to any page and you'll discover his distinctive style in the short, declarative sentences interspersed with long, rambling statements that often run for half a page. Children listen, recognize this powerful effect, then try to mimic it in their own writing pieces. Some of my favorite passages of *Charlotte's Web* are the book's final two paragraphs. This beautiful conclusion to a tale of the heartache, joys, and sorrows of a true friendship also provides writers with a great model for varying sentence structure and length to convey depth and meaning, and add poetry to one's storytelling.

Many classrooms have thematic units where the work of one author is explored for a week, a month, or longer. These units can also explore a theme—such as sibling relations/rivalry—using a variety of texts on the topic. In focusing specifically on style and voice with partners, a possible instructional progression might be as follows:

- The teacher shares literature and models what she sees/notices about an author's style or voice.
- The teacher shares literature and facilitates a student discussion, charting what writers see/notice about aspects of an author's style or voice.
- Writing partners explore examples of literature, taking notes and using sticky notes to highlight passages and ask questions.
- Writing partners share their findings about style and voice with the class and teacher and create charts or informational sheets outlining their findings.
- The teacher facilitates a shared writing activity, using partners' findings about style and voice to write a brief group writing piece aping an author's style or voice.
- Writing partners co-compose a longer piece using what they have learned about an author's style and voice to shape their writing.

Partners come up with amazing work during this kind of study. Rather than copy an author's style or voice, they usually take what they need and create writing that screams of their own personalities and style.

■ Using Literature to Explore Style and Voice

As with all the strategies in this book, there are many directions and pathways to take when exploring voice and style, and teachers will want to use literature models that suit their curriculum, student interests, and needs. I usually choose the writer for our first month of author study, then invite students to add names to a suggestion box if they would like to explore other authors. I use their ideas, but slip in my own favorite mentor texts, if they fit, during content area studies or literature units. Since ideas for textual exploration are limitless, you really cannot go wrong if you select quality literature to share and model.

Units, Books, and Authors

The example below offers one of my favorite thematic units and describes a few favorite books and authors for exploring style and voice.

Sibling relationships. There are hundreds of literature choices for this topic. Here are a few from authors, with a wide range of styles and voices:

- *Much Bigger Than Martin* (Kellogg 1976) In Kellogg's humorous tale, first-person narrator Henry, the little brother, imagines how much sweeter life would be if he were "much bigger" than bossy, big brother Martin. Kellogg's tale is a great model of ironic voice as well as the effective use of compare-and-contrast text structuring, as Henry moves from one imaginary scenario to the next. When his attempt to grow by eating dozens of apples makes him sick but no bigger, Martin's kindness in the face of Henry's distress provides a satisfying conclusion. In true Kellogg style, this is not quite the end of sibling ups and downs. The closing page finds Henry on a pair of stilts he has built to tower over Martin at last. Kellogg's droll style is very much in evidence here, along with his wonderful drawings that tell as much of the story as text. Pictures, in this case, are truly worth a thousand words!
- *Sisters* (McPhail 1984). In contrast to Kellogg's rollicking, boisterous style and ironic voice, McPhail tells a quieter tale of two sisters and how they are alike and different. A terrific model of a compare-and-contrast style of storytelling as well as the power of a hushed, familiar voice.

- *The Trouble with Jack* (Hughes 1970). Hughes' story of family life accompanied by her soft, realistic illustrations is a great model of fiction for partners wanting to explore this genre or a tale of domestic life, told with strong verbs, effectively used dialogue, and just the right amount of description to move plot along. Poor older sister Nancy has to put up with little brother Jack. He makes messes, he gets into things, and nearly spoils his big sister's birthday celebration. But, his warm, loving family always forgives him— even his exasperated big sister. "The trouble with Jack," Nancy says at the story's end, "is that as he's my brother I've got to put up with him whatever he's like." Isn't that the way with little brothers (and sisters)?
- *The Baby Sister* (dePaola 1996). Unlike the other three, this "story" is autobiographical and tells of the author's experiences as he awaits the arrival of his new baby sister, Maureen. Told with humor and a clear, episodic plot, children of all ages make connections to this story and events of their own lives. Tomie dePaola gives them ideas and devices to tell their own stories, including what's taking place in the story and what's happening in the main character's head. Writing partners can read and reread this story, asking each other:
  - How does the author convey Tommy's anxiety?
  - How did the ending relieve the reader's and main character's anxiety?

Partners can also explore a nonfiction account of the author's life in Barbara Elleman's *Tomie dePaola: His Art and His Stories* (1999) and find photographs of Tomie and his sister, Maureen, as children and adults, opening readers eyes to the countless stories awaiting to emerge from everyday lives, even their own.

Using Poetry to Explore Voice and Style

Poetry makes a wonderful vehicle through which to research and explore voice and style. Taking the next step—emulating or copying the poet's voice and style—is sometimes less daunting than attempting the same with longer, more complex prose. Among the many poets I use in exploring poetic style are:

- Shel Silverstein
- Jack Prelutsky
- Eve Merriman
- Lee Bennett Hopkins
- Karla Kuskin
- Dr. Seuss
- Judith Viorst

The list goes on and on!

Encapsulating Story: Writing Strong, Evocative Introductions

I love the two opening paragraphs of Patricia MacLachlan's *Sarah, Plain and Tall* (1985); they tell so much with so little. In under fifty words, we meet two motherless siblings—older sister Anna, the narrator, and little brother Caleb, who never ceases to ask about the mother he never knew—"for the second time this week. For the twentieth time this month. The hundredth time this year? And the past few years?" (3). Anna's sorrow lingers beneath her words and her exasperated replies to Caleb's relentless questioning about her beloved mother. Look for books and stories where the author does this kind of masterful "encapsulating." Nothing draws the reader in like a great lead, and not many do it better than MacLachlan.

Exploring Voice, Style, and Setting

I use two books—*Grandfather Twilight* (Berger 1984) and *The Relatives Came* (Rylant 1985)—to compare and contrast authors' voice and use of stylistic devices to tell the soft, quiet bedtime tale of *Grandfather Twilight* or describe the wild hysteria that ensues with the arrival of the Virginia relatives. Partners reading these stories can ask themselves whether they want to tell a story that flies screeching along like a freight train or meanders quietly like a burbling brook in the midsummer heat.

Exploring Rhyme, Rhythm, and Beautiful Language

There are so many books from which to choose in exploring the lyrical qualities of text. A model young readers enjoy is *Good Night, Good Knight* (Thomas 2000), the story of three lonely little dragons in their deep, dark cave who roar out for help and are answered by the kind knight who descends his crumbly tumbly tower to gallop, "Clippety-clop, Clippety-clop," through the forest to the rescue. Thomas' book is easy to read and has a clear, recognizable style and tone that children enjoy playing with and copying. Plus, it tells a sweet, humorous story ending with the knight bestowing goodnight kisses on each little scaly dragon cheek. Other favorites of mine for exploring rhyme, rhythm, and beautiful language are:

1. Anything by Mem Fox! Two of my favorite, are:
   * *Wilfred Gordon MacDonald Partridge* (1985)
   * *Koala Lou* (1988)
2. *Moon Man* (Ungerer 1998). Imagination soars as we begin the tale of Moon Man, curled up in his "shimmering seat in space" (1).

3. Anything by Ruth Heller! Factual information sails off the page, captivating hearts and minds in such tales as:
   - *Chickens Aren't the Only Ones* (1981)
4. *Chicka Chicka Boom Boom* (Martin and Archambault 1989). Need I say more?
5. *A House Is a House for Me* (Hoberman 1978). Just typing the title starts my toes tapping!

■ Questions to Begin Exploring Style and Voice

When preparing my first graders for writing animal reports, I examine and discuss many styles of nonfiction literature, author voice, and text formats. We talk about what grabs our attention and what kinds of devices and strategies authors use to keep us reading. Betsy was fascinated by Ruth Heller's style, and she particularly loved the book *Chickens Aren't the Only Ones* (Heller 1981). After reading the book many times, she used Heller's stylistic device of questioning the reader in her beaver report. In *Chickens Aren't the Only Ones*, two seahorses are depicted. The text reads

This mother SEAHORSE
lays her eggs
into the
father's pouch.
He keeps
them there
until they
hatch, and
then he's
through.

I think
that's
nice
of him,
don't you? (23)

After studying Heller's books, Betsy began her report on beavers with this opening paragraph:

A beaver builds a den to keep warm. They cut down trees to build a den. I think they're cute. Don't you?

When focusing on style and voice, we want writing buddies and individual writers to look carefully at mentor texts as Betsy has done. We want writers to develop and ask good questions about what distinguishes a particular author from another. So they can recognize style and voice when they read. Teachers may want to take time to develop some of the following questions with writing partners sending them off to explore:

- Does the author repeat words or phrases? How does that impact how we read him or her?
- How do we learn about the characters? Do we learn through the author's descriptions? Dialogue? Characters' actions and behaviors?
- Does the author vary sentences, paragraphs, or page length? How does this affect the reader?
- How does an author use different kinds of sentences—statements, questions, and exclamations—to get particular effects or produce particular reactions for readers?
- Does the author use strong verbs?
- How does the author convey humor?
- How important are the illustrations? What would be lost without them?
- What about text signals—bold text, italics, capital letters, punctuation? How do these affect the sound and pace of text?
- What makes a book loud or quiet? How does an author convey this in words?
- What makes us want to read the text slowly or fast?

These kinds of questions lead partners deeper into style and voice so that when they begin writing, emulating an author's voice or copying his particular writing style, they have a road map of sorts of the qualities identified during their explorations.

■ Moving Toward Independence

Just as with other strategies outlined in this book, individuals bring insights and knowledge discovered in partner explorations of style and voice to their independent writing efforts. With their partner, they may have compromised to shape the collective, mutually agreed-on voice, or, more likely, created pieces characterized by two voices and two styles as children shared the pen. Sharing, while supportive in building individuals' skills and conceptual knowledge, can be frustrating for writers who long to do it "my way." Moving this strategy to independent writing is the perfect solution for partners' desires because it allows each individual, with specific intentions and plans, to craft a piece that reflects her own unique, well-reasoned style and clearer, more distinctive voice.

■ Suggestions for English Language Learners

The suggestions for minilessons given below can benefit all students, but may be particularly supportive of English language learners as they grapple with the idea of author voice and style while still struggling to learn language, vocabulary and concepts.

1. *Teacher's Writing Models.* The teacher models examples of her personal writing with students, making explicit connections to authors who have influenced her style and voice. The more explicit we can be in showing how our own writing mirrors specific passages borrowed from an author's style or voice, the more helpful it will be to young writers, especially, ELL writers.

2. *About the Authors.* Every year, new author biographies are published for readers of all ages. The Internet is also a rich source of information. Many children's authors have their own websites as well as numerous others devoted to their writing and their lives. Reading about how professional writers manage their routines, writing process, research, and daily life gives children clues to how authors' voice and style originate and how these qualities continue to develop as they live and write.

3. *Group sharing of writers' own style and voice.* Children can share what they know about their own style and voice, making connections to authors and to aspects of their world that have influenced their writing. Children typically love to do this kind of sharing. It is a great way to begin and conclude a specific writing focus unit or period of study on style and voice and gives ELL writers a way to share their culture and language while learning about the English language.

Strategy Bookmark Template

WAYS TO HELP MY PARTNER	RULES FOR OUR PARTNERSHIP

Genre Research Form

Names_____   _____

Date_____   **Title** _____

What we notice about _____ . . .
(genre under study)

Notes

Comments and Criteria

_____

_____

_____

Books to Focus on Aspects of Narrative

On any given day, this list grows and changes depending on my current favorites. It is a mix of old and new and represents a tiny sampling of what's out there. Teachers should select and use literature that touches their hearts and best illustrates characterization, plot, setting, and tone. The choices are many!

■ Focus on Characterization

ALLARD, HARRY, AND JAMES MARSHALL. 1977. *Miss Nelson Is Missing*. Boston: Houghton Mifflin.

BRONIN, ANDREW. 1975. *Gus and Buster Work Things Out*. New York: Dell.

CANNON, JANELL. 1993. *Stellaluna*. New York: Harcourt.

COONEY, MARGARET. 1994. *Only Opal: The Diary of a Young Girl*. New York: Scholastic.

ELSTER, J. ALICIA. 1977. *Just call me Joe*. Valley Forge, PA: Judson Press.

HENKES, KEVIN. 1989. *Jessica*. New York: Puffin Books.

HOFFMAN, MARY. 1995. *Boundless Grace*. New York: Scholastic.

KEATS, EZRA JACK. 1968. *A Letter to Amy*. New York: Harper & Row.

KILBORNE, SARAH, S. 1994. *Peach and Blue*. New York: Alfred A. Knopf.

LIONNI, LEO. 1973. *Swimmy*. New York: Pinwheel.

MACLACHLAN, PATRICIA. 1980. *Through Grandpa's Eyes*. New York: HarperCollins.

MUNSCH, ROBERT. 2001. *The Paper Bag Princess*. New York: Annick Press.

PALACCO, PATRICIA. 1990. *Babushka's Doll*. New York: Alladin Books.

———. 1994. *My Rotten Redheaded Older Brother*. New York: Simon & Schuster for Young Readers.

———. 1994. *Pink and Say*. New York: Philomel Books.

SHANNON, DAVID. 1998. *A Bad Case of Stripes*. New York: Scholastic.

———. 1998. *No, David!* New York: Scholastic.

STEIG, WILLIAM. 1971. *Amos and Boris*. New York: Puffin.

SEUSS, DR. 1940. *Horton Hatches the Egg*. New York: Random House.

———. 1950. *Yertle the Turtle and Other Stories*. New York: Random House.

■ Focus on Plot

AVI. 1999. *Abigail Takes the Wheel*. New York: HarperCollins.

EDWARDS, PAMELA DUNCAN. 1997. *Dinorella: A Prehistoric Fairy Tale*. New York: Scholastic.

EMBERLEY, REBECCA. 1995. *Three Cool Kids*. Boston: Little Brown.

GIFF, PATRICIA REILLY. 1980. *Today Was a Terrible Day*. New York: Puffin.

GREEN, NORMA. 1974. *A Hole in the Dike*. New York: Scholastic.

HAYES, JOE. 1996. *A Spoon for Every Bite*. New York: Orchard Books.

HUTCHINS, PAT. 1968. *Rosie's Walk*. New York: Puffin Books.

———. 1986. *The Doorbell Rang*. New York: Scholastic.

LEWIS, KIM. 1995. *My Friend Harry*. London: Walker Books.

LOBEL, ARNOLD. 1969. *Small Pig*. New York: HarperCollins.

———. 1970. *Frog and Toad Are Friends*. New York: HarperCollins.

———. 1976 *Frog and Toad All Year*. New York: Scholastic.

———. 1980. *Fables*. New York: HarperCollins.

———. 1979. *Days with Frog and Toad*. New York: HarperCollins.

O'CONNOR, JANE. 1986. *The Teeny Tiny Woman*. New York: Random House.

RYLANT, CYNTHIA. Cobblestreet Cousins series: New York: Scholastic Books.

———. 1994. *Henry and Mudge: Book 1*. New York: Scholastic Books.

SCIESZKA, JON. 1991. *The Frog Prince Revisited*. New York: Scholastic.

WABER, BERNARD. 1972. *Ira Sleeps Over*. New York: Houghton Mifflin.

YOLEN, JANE. 1992. *Encounter*. New York: Voyager Books.

■ Focus on Setting

ARADEMA, VERA. 1981. *Bringing the Rain to Kapiti Plain*. New York: Scholastic.

BAYLOR, BYRD. 1978. *The Way to Start a Day*. New York: Alladin.

DORROS, ARTHUR. 1991. *Abuela*. New York: Trumpet Books.

FRENCH, FIONA. 1986. *Snow White in New York*. Toronto, ON: Oxford University Press.

LAVERDE, ARLENE. 2000. *Alaska's Three Little Pigs*. Seattle, WA: Sasquatch Books.

MURPHY, CLAIRE RUDOLF, AND JANE G. HAIGH. 2001. *Children of the Gold Rush*. Portland, OR: Alaska Northwest Books.

SENDAK, MAURICE. 1970. *In the Night Kitchen*. New York: HarperCollins.

WILLIAMS, VERA. 1982. *A Chair for My Mother*. New York: Mulberry.

◼ Focus on Tone

Alphabet Books

KREEGER, CHARLENE, AND SHANNON CARTWRIGHT. 1978. *Alaska A B C Book*. Seattle, WA: Sasquatch Books.

LESTER, MIKE. 2000. *A Is for Salad*. New York: Putnam & Grosset.

ROSE, DEBORAH LEE. 2000. *Into the A, B, Sea*. New York: Scholastic.

Other Books

BAYLOR, BYRD. 1974. *Everybody Needs a Rock*. New York: Simon & Schuster.

BROWNE, ANTHONY. 1990. *Changes*. London: Walker Books.

GREENFIELD, ELOISE. 1988. *Nathaniel Talking*. New York: Black Butterfly Children's Books.

LITTLEFIELD HOOPES, LYN. 1997. *Condor Magic*. Fairfield, CT: The Benefactory.

PARKER, BETH. 1990. *Thomas just Knew There Were Pirates in the Bathroom*. WINDSOR, ON: Black Moss.

PERLMAN, JANET. 1992. *Cinderella Penquin*. New York: Scholastic.

SENDAK, MAURICE. 1970. *In the Night Kitchen*. New York: HarperCollins.

VAMEY, SUSAN. 1984. *Badger's Parting Gifts*. New York: Mulberry.

VIORST, JUDITH. 1990. Earrings! New York: Alladin.

———. 1971. *The Tenth Good Thing About Barney*. New York: Alladin.

YOLEN, JANE. 1972. *The Girl Who Loved the Wind*. New York: Harper & Row.

We Edit: Partners Editing Checklist

Names_____

Title_____ Writer_____

Genre_____ Date _____

	Writers	
Spelling	1	2

I/we . . .
- Found words that don't look right · ☐ ☐
- Checked for "tricky words" ☐ ☐
- Used the dictionary or other resource ☐ ☐

Comments_____

Does It Make Sense?

I/we . . .
- Checked to see if words or parts were missing ☐ ☐
- Checked sentences—were they too long? Confusing? ☐ ☐
- Read and retold to the writer to make sure of understanding ☐ ☐

Comments_____

Punctuation

I/we . . .
- Checked for **periods, commas, question marks,** and **exclamation marks** ☐ ☐
- Checked for **uppercase letters** to begin each sentence, and proper nouns ☐ ☐

Comments_____

Other Editing Considerations

I/we . . .
- Checked for indented paragraphs ☐ ☐
- Checked for legible handwriting ☐ ☐
- Discussed what was needed before publishing ☐ ☐

Comments_____

Peer Revising and Questioning Form

Writer_____ **Editor/Reader**_____

Title _____ **Date** _____

What can the writer tell me?

1. How can I help you?

2. What should I be listening for?

3. Why did you choose to write this piece?

4. Did your idea work out when you wrote it down?

5. What was easy about writing this piece?

6. What was difficult? Can I help with this?

7. What are the most important parts of this piece? Is there more you can tell me about these parts?

8. What is your plan for this piece?

9. What is your plan for your next piece?

COMMENTS and FEEDBACK:_____

_____

Peer Response Form

Writer _____   **Editor/Reader** _____

Title _____   **Date** _____

What can I share with the writer?

1. Parts that interested me

2. How the writing made me think

3. How the writing made me feel

4. Where I was confused

5. What I'm wondering about

6. Where I want to know more

7. Where I heard the writer's voice

8. Where I noticed the author's style

9. What I suggest (based on what the writer tells me she needs)_____

_____

I Imagine . . .

Names _____

I imagine _____

ECHO

I imagine _____

ECHO

I imagine_____

ECHO

I imagine _____

We imagine _____

We imagine _____

We imagine _____

We imagine _____

People Poem Format

Line 1:   Person's name

Line 2:   Three or four words (adjectives) that describe her

Line 3:   Five to six words (nouns) that tell about "who" the character is (e.g., brother, artist, etc.)

Line 4:   Cares about (three things)

Line 5:   Feels (three emotions)

Line 6:   Needs (three things)

Line 7:   Shares (three things)

Line 8:   Fears (three things)

Line 9:   Whose favorite clothing is (three things)

Line 10:   Who wishes (finish the sentence)

Line 11:   Lives (tell where person lives, such as town or street name, state, or geographic locale like "by the shore")

Line 12:   Repeat line 1

People Poem Grid

Names _____   **Date** _____

Line 1: _____

Line 2: _____

Line 3: _____

Line 4: _____

Line 5: _____

Line 6: _____

Line 7: _____

Line 8: _____

Line 9: _____

Line 10: _____

Line 11: _____

Line 12: _____

Expectations Sentences

Expectations we have about _____

1. We have _____

2. We do not expect _____

3. They are _____

4. They are not _____

5. Sometimes they will _____

6. Sometimes they will not _____

7. They always _____

8. They sometimes _____

9. They never _____

Other thoughts _____

Words We Might Find In . . .

Title _____   **Date** _____

Names _____

Words we might find are . . .

WORD	YES	NO
1. _____	_____	_____
2. _____	_____	_____
3. _____	_____	_____
4. _____	_____	_____
5. _____	_____	_____
6. _____	_____	_____
7. _____	_____	_____
8. _____	_____	_____
9. _____	_____	_____
10. _____	_____	_____

Comments and Surprises: _____

_____

Partner Names _____   **Date** _____

How's It Going?

How's it going with partner writing?

What have we learned together?

What ideas, strategies, and tools can we share with others?

Partner Names _____ **Date** _____

Character Map

What we noticed about a character . . .

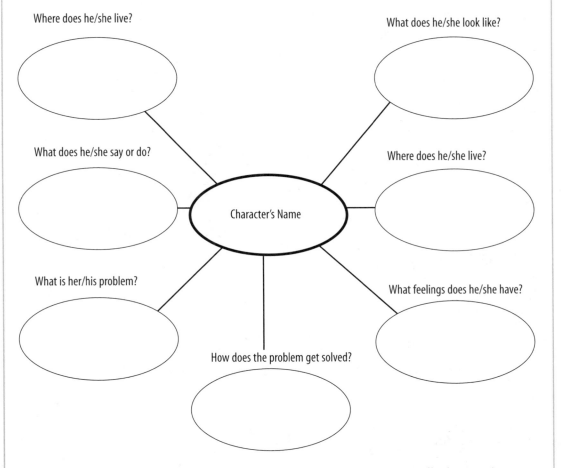

Where does he/she live?

What does he/she look like?

What does he/she say or do?

Where does he/she live?

Character's Name

What is her/his problem?

What feelings does he/she have?

How does the problem get solved?

From _Writer to Writer_. Portsmouth, NH: Heinemann. © 2005 by Mary Lee Prescott-Griffin from _Reader to Reader_. Portsmouth, NH: Heinemann.

Partner Names _____ **Date** _____

Character Planning

Questions about this character * in our story . . .

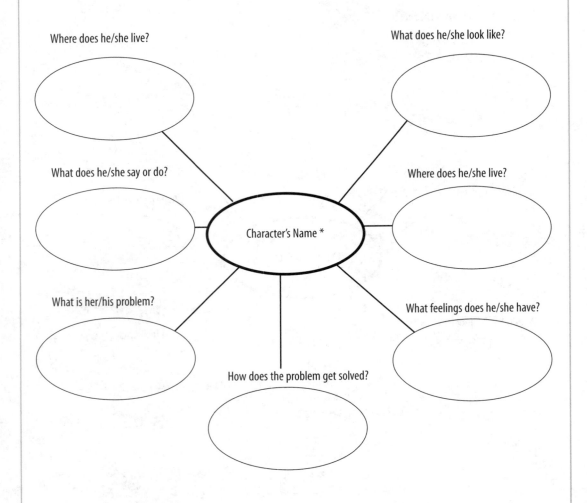

Where does he/she live?

What does he/she look like?

What does he/she say or do?

Where does he/she live?

Character's Name *

What is her/his problem?

What feelings does he/she have?

How does the problem get solved?

Partner Names _____ Date _____

Comparing Characters

How are they are alike and/or different?

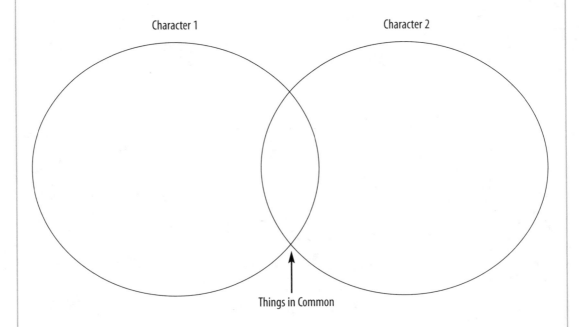

Character 1   Character 2

Things in Common

Partner Names _____ **Date** _____

Comparing Characters

How are these characters alike and/or different?

Character 1   Character 2

Things in Common

Story Planning Circle

Our story from beginning to end . . .

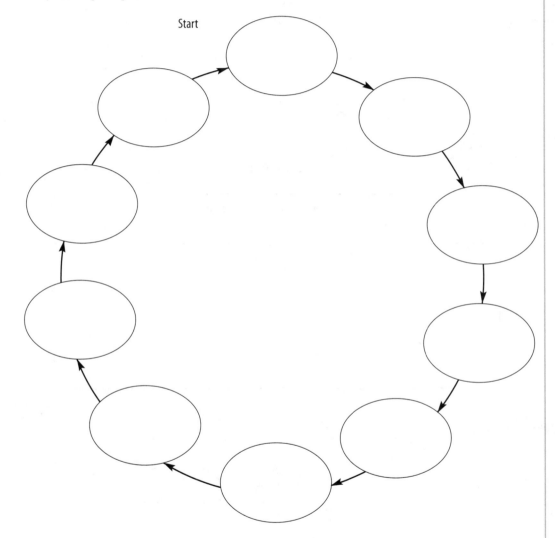

Start

Narrative "GO Chart"

Names _____

Date _____ **Title** _____

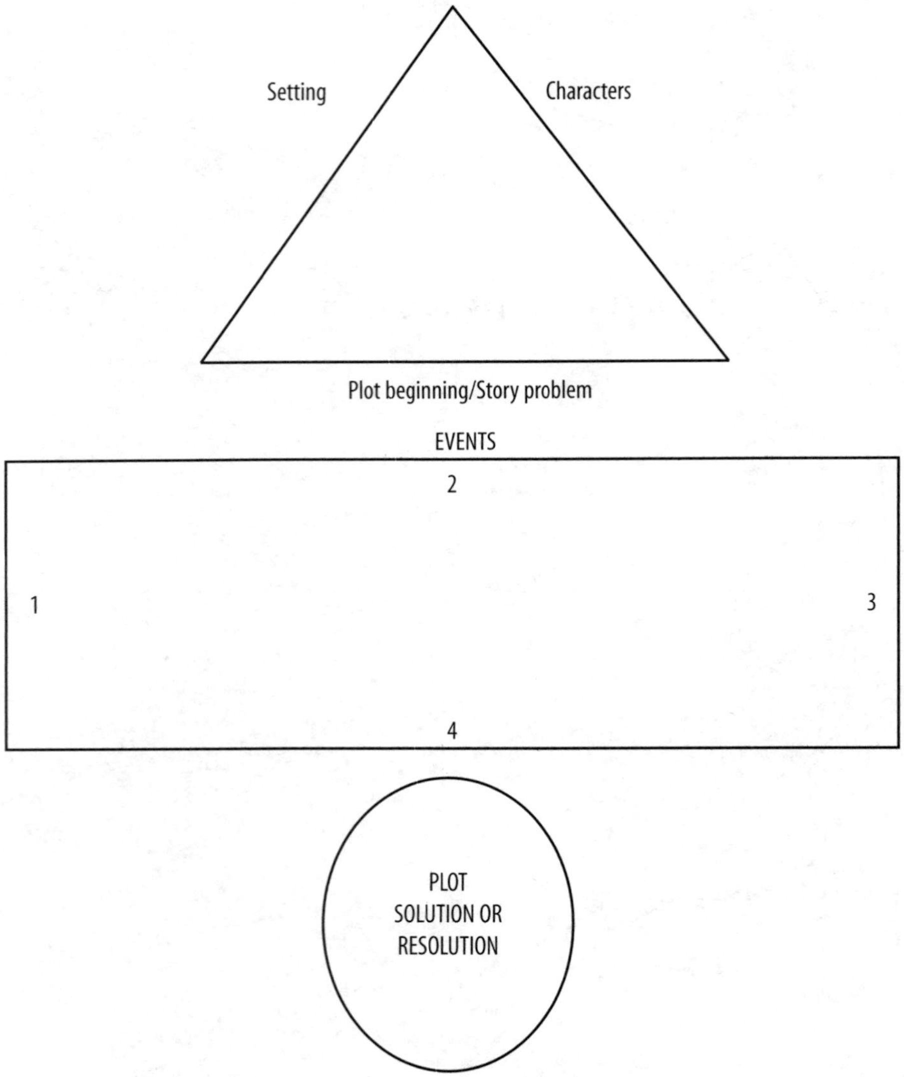

Setting   Characters

Plot beginning/Story problem

EVENTS

2

1   3

4

PLOT
SOLUTION OR
RESOLUTION

Partner Names _____ Date _____

Web of Information

Draw and write about your topic. Start your web in the middle and branch out! Be sure to add extra branches as needed.

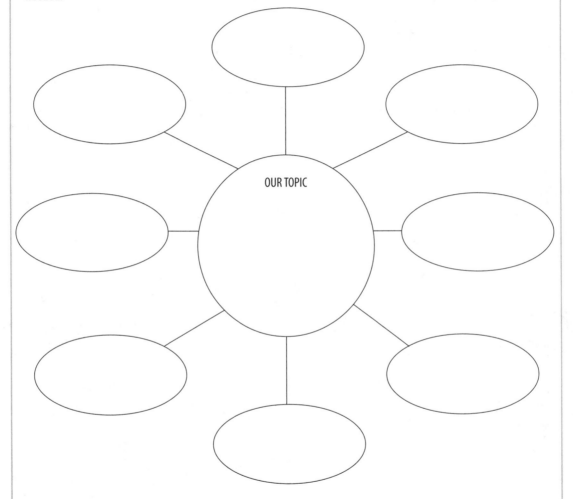

Partner Names _____ **Date** _____

K-W-L Chart

What we KNOW, WANT to know, and what my partner and I LEARNED from our research.

K	W	L
WHAT WE *KNOW*	WHAT WE *WANT* TO KNOW	WHAT WE *LEARNED*

From *Writer to Writer*. Portsmouth, NH: Heinemann. © 2005 by Mary Lee Prescott-Griffin from *Reader to Reader*. Portsmouth, NH: Heinemann.

Children's Literature Cited

ADA, ALMA FLOR. 1998. *Yours Truly, Goldilocks*. New York: Aladdin Paperbacks.

AHLBERG, ALLAN, AND JANET ALHBERG 1986. *The Jolly Postman: Or Other People's Letters*. Boston: Little, Brown.

ALLARD, HARRY, AND JAMES MARSHALL. 1977. *Miss Nelson Is Missing*. Boston: Houghton Mifflin.

BERGER, BARBARA. 1984. *Grandfather Twilight*. New York: Scholastic.

BRETT, J. 1981. *Fritz and the Beautiful Horses*. Boston: Houghton Mifflin.

———. 1989. *The Mitten*. New York: G. P. Putnam's Sons.

———. 1996. *Comet's Nine Lives*. New York: Scholastic.

DEEDRICK, TAMI. 1998. *Astronauts*. Community Helpers Series. Mankato, MN: Capstone Press.

DEPAOLA, TOMIE. 1975. *STREGA NONA*. Upper Saddle River, NJ: Prentice Hall.

———. 1978. *Bill and Pete*. New York: G. P. Putnam's Sons.

———. 1983. *The Legend of the Bluebonnet: An Old Tale of Texas*. New York: G. P. Putnam's Sons.

———. 1996. *The Baby Sister*. New York: Penguin Putnam.

FOX, MEM. 1985. *Wilfred Gordon MacDonald Partridge*. New York: Kane/Miller.

———. 1988. *Koala Lou*. New York: Harcourt Brace.

GARLAND, SHERRY. 1993. *The Lotus Seed*. New York: Harcourt, Brace.

HELLER, RUTH. 1981. *Chickens Aren't the Only Ones*. New York: Grosset & Dunlap.

HOBERMAN, MARY ANN. 1978. *A House Is a House for Me*. New York: Viking.

HUGHES, SHIRLEY. 1970. *The trouble with Jack*. London: Red Fox Books.

———. 1978. *Moving Molly*. London: Red Fox Books.

————. 1988. *Dogger*. New York: Mulberry Books.

KEATS, EZRA JACK. 1962. *The Snowy Day*. New York: Scholastic.

KELLOGG, STEVEN. 1976. *Much Bigger Than Martin*. New York: The Dial Press.

LAMARCHE, JIM. 2000. *The Raft*. New York: HarperCollins.

LESTER, ALLISON. 1989. *Imagine*. Boston: Houghton Mifflin.

MACLACHLAN, PATRICIA. 1985. *Sarah, Plain and Tall*. New York: Harper & Row.

MCNAUGHTON, COLIN. 1994. *Suddenly*. New York: HarperCollins.

MARTIN, BILL. 1983. *Brown Bear, Brown Bear, What Do You See?* New York: Henry Holt.

MARTIN, BILL, AND JOHN ARCHAMBAULT. 1989. *Chicka Chicka Boom Boom*. New York: Simon & Schuster.

MCPHAIL, DAVID. 1984. *Sisters*. New York: Harcourt Brace.

MYERS, BERNICE. 1985. *Sidney Rella and the Glass Sneaker*. New York: Macmillan.

PEET, BILL. 1971. *How Droofus the Dragon Lost His Head*. Boston: Houghton Mifflin.

PINKWATER, DANIEL MANUS. 1977. *The Big Orange Splot*. New York: Scholastic.

OAKLEY, GRAHAM. 1978. *The Church Mice at Bay*. New York: Atheneum.

————. 1981. *Hetty and Harriet*. New York: Atheneum.

READY, DEE. 1997. *Nurses* Community Helpers Series. Mankato, MN: Capstone Press.

ROJANKOVSKY, F. (illustrator). 1944. The Tall Book of Nursery Tales. New York: Harper & Row.

RYLANT, CYNTHIA. 1985. *The relatives came*. New York: Bradbury Press.

SCIESZKA, JON. 1989. *The True Story of the Three Little Pigs*. New York: Viking.

SWOPE, SAM. 1989. *The Araboolies of Liberty Street*. New York: Farrar, Straus & Giroux.

THOMAS, S. M. 2000. *Good Night, Good Knight*. New York: Dutton Children's Books.

UNGERER, TOMI. 1998. *Moon Man*. London: Roberts Rinehart.

WHITE, E. B. 1952. *Charlotte's Web*. New York: HarperCollins.

ZOLOTOW, CHARLOTTE. (1965). *Someday*. New York: Harper & Row.

References

APPLEBEE, A. N. 1996. *Curriculum as Conversation: Transforming Traditions of Teaching and Learning.* Chicago: University of Chicago Press.

ATWELL, N. 1985. "Writing and Reading from the Inside out." In J. Hansen, T. Newkirk, and D. Graves, eds., *Breaking Ground: Teachers Relate Reading and Writing in the Elementary Years.* Portsmouth, NH: Heinemann.

———. 1987. "Building a Dining Room Table: Dialogue Journals About Reading." In T. Fulwiler, ed. *The Journal Book,* 157–70. Portsmouth, NH: Boynton/Cook Heinemann.

BARNES, D. 1992. *From Communication to Curriculum.* Portsmouth, NH: Heinemann.

———. 1995. "Talking and Learning in Classrooms: An Introduction." *Primary Voices K–6,* 3: 16–29.

BRADY, S., AND S. JACOBS. 1994. *Mindful of Others: Teaching Children to Teach.* Portsmouth, NH: Heinemann.

BROMLEY, K. D. 1991. *Webbing with Literature: Creating Story Maps with Children's Books.* Boston: Allyn & Bacon.

CALKINS, L. M. 1994. *The Art of Teaching Writing.* Portsmouth, NH: Heinemann.

CICALESE, C. 2003. Children's Perspectives on Interactive Writing versus Independent Writing in Primary Grades. Educational Resources Information Center (ERIC) M.A. research project, Kean University.

CONDON, M. W. F., AND J. A. CLYDE. 1996. "Co-authoring: Composing Through Conversation." *Language Arts* 73: 587–96.

COOK-GUMPERZ, J., ed. 1986. *The Social Construction of Literacy.* Cambridge, UK: Cambridge University Press.

CUMMINS, J. 2001. *Language, Power and Pedagogy: Bilingual Children in the Crossfire.* Clevedon, UK: Multilingual Matters.

DANIELS, H., AND M. BIZAR. 1998. *Methods That Matter: Six Structures for Best Practice Classrooms.* Portland, ME: Stenhouse.

D'ARCY, P. 1987. "Writing to Learn." In T. Fulwiler, ed. *The Journal Book*, 41–46. Portsmouth, NH: Boynton/Cook Heinemann.

DAVIS, J., AND S. HILL. 2003. *The No-Nonsense Guide to Teaching Writing: Strategies, Structures and Solutions*. Portsmouth, NH: Heinemann.

DEWEY, J. 1938. *Experience and Education*. New York: Collier.

DOUGLAS, W. W. 1972. "An American View of the Failure of Curriculum Reform and the Way Ahead." *English in Education* 6 (2): 5–18.

DYSON, A. H. 1983. "The Role of Oral Language in Early Writing Processes." *Research in the Teaching of English* 17 (1): 1–30.

———. 1993. *Social Worlds of Children Learning to Write in an Urban School*. New York: Teachers College Press.

EDELSKY, C., AND K. JILBERT. 1985. "Bilingual Children and Writing Lessons for All of Us." *Volta Review* 87 (5): 57–72.

ELLEMAN, B. 1999. *Tomie dePaola: His Art and His Stories*. New York: Putnam.

FLETCHER, R. 1993. *What a Writer Needs*. Portsmouth, NH: Heinemann.

FLETCHER, R., AND J. PORTALUPI. 1998. *Craft Lessons: Teaching Writing, K–8*. Portland, ME: Stenhouse.

———. 2001. *Nonfiction Craft Lessons: Teaching Informational Writing, K–8*. Portland, ME: Stenhouse.

FOSNOT, C., ed. 1996. *Constructivism: Theory, Perspectives and Practice*. New York: Teachers College Press.

FULWILER, T., ed. 1987. *The Journal Book*. Portsmouth, NH: Boynton/Cook Heinemann.

GARCIA, R. L. 1974. "Mexican Americans Learn Through Language Experience." *The Reading Teacher* 28 (4): 301–5.

GORDON, T. 2000. *Parent Effectiveness Training*. Three Rivers, MI: Three Rivers Press.

GRAVES, D. 1983. *Writing: Teachers and Children at Work*. Portsmouth, NH: Heinemann.

GRIFFIN, M. L. 2001. "Social Contexts of Beginning Reading." *Language Arts* 78 (4): 371–78.

———. 2002. "'Why Don't You Use Your Finger?' Paired Reading in First Grade." *The Reading Teacher* 55 (8): 766–74.

HADAWAY, N. L. 1990. "Writing partnerships: Teaching ESL Composition Through Letter Exchanges." *The Writing Notebook* 8 (1): 10–12.

HADAWAY, N., S. VERDELL, AND T. YOUNG. 2002. *Literature-Based Instruction with English Language Learners*. Boston: Allyn & Bacon.

HALL, N., AND A. ROBINSON, eds. 1994. *Keeping in Touch: Using Interactive Writing with Young Children*. London: Hodder & Stoughton.

HARVEY, S., AND A. GOUDVIS. 2000. *Strategies That Work: Teaching Comprehension to Enhance Understanding*. Portland, ME: Stenhouse.

HARWAYNE, S. 2001. *Writing Through Childhood: Rethinking Process and Product*. Portsmouth, NH: Heinemann.

HEARD, G. 2002. *The Revision Toolbox: Teaching Techniques That Work*. Portsmouth, NH: Heinemann.

Hoyt, Linda. 2000. *Snapshots: Literacy Minilessons Up Close*. Portsmouth, NH: Heinemann.

Hudelson, S. 1983. Janice: Becoming a Writer of English. Paper presented at the Seventeenth Annual Meeting of Teachers of English to Speakers of Other Languages. Toronto, Ontario.

————. 1989. *Write On: Children Writing Is ESL*. Englewood Cliffs, NJ: Prentice Hall Regents.

Jagger, A. M., D. H. Carrara, and S. E. Weiss. 1986. "Research Currents: The Influence of Reading on Children's Narrative Writing (and Vica Versa)." *Language Arts* 63 (3): 292–300.

Johnson, D. M., and D. H. Roen, eds. 1989. *Richness in Writing: Empowering ESL Students*. New York: Longman.

Kagan, S. 1992. *Cooperative Learning*. San Juan Capistrano, CA: Kagan Cooperative Learning.

Keene, E. O., and S. Zimmerman. 1997. *Mosaic of Thought: Teaching Comprehension in a Reader's Workshop*. Portsmouth, NH: Heinemann.

Kooy, M., and J. Wells. 1996. *Reading Response Logs: Inviting Students to Explore Novels, Short Stories, Plays, Poetry and More*. Markham, ONt: Pembroke.

Lado, A. 2006. Stories to Read Aloud: Teaching English Language Learners with Themed Books. Talk given at the International Reading Convention, Chicago, Illinois.

Lancia, P. J. 1997. "Literary Borrowing: The Effects of Literature on Children's Writing." *The Reading Teacher* 50 (6): 470–75.

MacGillivray, L. 1997. "'I've Seen You Read': Reading Strategies in a First-Grade Class." *Journal of Research in Childhood Education* 11 (2): 135–46.

MacGillivray, L. and S. Hawes. 1994. "'I Don't Know What I'm Doing—They All Start with B': First Graders Negotiate Peer Reading Interactions." *The Reading Teacher* 48 (3): 210–17.

McCauley, J., and D. McCauley. 1992. "Using Choral Reading to Promote Language Learning for ESL Students." *The Reading Teacher* 39: 206–12.

McMackin, M. C., and B. S. Siegel. 2002. *Knowing How: Researching and Writing Nonfiction*, 3–8. Portland, ME: Stenhouse.

Moll, L. C., and S. Diaz. 1993. "Change as the Goal of Educational Research." In E. Jacob and C. Jordan, eds, *Minority Education: Anthropological Perspectives*, 66–79. Norwood, NJ: Ablex.

Moss, J. 1984. *Focus Units in Literature: A Handbook for Elementary School Teachers*. Urbana, IL: National Council of Teachers of English.

————. 1990. *Focus on Literature: A Context for Literacy Learning*. Katonah, New York: Richard C. Owen.

Opitz, M. F., and T. V. Rasinski. 1998. *Good-Bye Round Robin: Twenty-Five Effective Oral Reading Strategies*. Portsmouth, NH: Heinemann.

Ovando, C. J., M. C. Combs, and V. P. Collier. 2006. *Bilingual and ESL Classrooms: Teaching in Multicultural Contexts*. Boston: McGraw-Hill.

Nelson, O. G., and W. M. Linek. 1999. *Practical Classroom Applications of Language Experience: Looking Back, Looking Forward*. Boston: Allyn & Bacon.

Nia, I. T. 1999. "Units of Study in the Writing Workshop." *Primary Voices K–6* 8 (1): 3–11.

Parsons, L. 1994. *Expanding Response Journals in All Subject Areas*. Portsmouth, NH: Heinemann.

Peyton, J. K., ed. 1990. *Students and Teachers Writing Together: Perspectives on Journal Writing*. Alexandria, VA: Teachers of English to Speakers of Other Languages.

Peyton, J. K., and L. Reed. 1990. *Dialogue Journal Writing with Nonnative English Speakers: A Handbook for Teachers*. Alexandria, VA: Teachers of English to Speakers of Other Languages.

Piaget, P. 1976. *The Grasp of Consciousness: Action and Concept in the Young Child.* Cambridge, MA: Harvard University Press.

Prescott-Griffin, M. L. 2004. "Using Peer Partnerships to Scaffold Reading." In A. Rodgers and E. Rodgers, eds., *Scaffolding Literacy Instruction: Strategies for K–4 Classrooms*. Portsmouth, NH: Heinemann. 121–42.

———. 2005a. *Reader to Reader: Building Independence in Peer Partnerships*. Portsmouth, NH: Heinemann.

———. 2005b. "Writing Partnerships: Building Strategies and Independence Together," *The Primer*. 33 (2).

Prescott-Griffin, M. L., and N. Witherell. 2004. *Fluency in Focus: Comprehension Strategies for Young Readers*. Portsmouth, NH: Heinemann.

Rose, M. 1989. *Live on the Boundary: A Moving Account of the Struggles and Achievements of America's Educationally Underprepared*. New York: Penguin Books.

Routman, R. 2000. *Conversations: Strategies for Teaching, Learning, and Evaluating*. Portsmouth, NH: Heinemann.

Rowe, D. 1994. *Preschoolers as Authors: Literacy Learning in the Social World of the Classroom*. Cresskill, NJ: Hampton Press.

Samway, K. D. 2006. *When English Language Learners Write*. Portsmouth, NH: Heinemann.

Sebesta, S. 1994. "The Benefits of Theme-Based Literature." In *Celebrate Reading: Professional Resources*. Carrollton, TX: Scott Foresman.

Short, D. 1991. *How to Integrate Language and Content Instruction: A Training Manual*. Washington, DC: Center for Applied Linguistics.

Smith, F. 1982. *Writing and the Writer.* New York: Holt, Rinehart and Winston.

Spandel, V. 2001. *Books, Lessons, Ideas for Teaching the Six Traits: Writing in the Elementary and Middle Grades*. Wilmington, MA: Great Source Educational Group.

Sprangenberg-Urbschat, K., and R. Pritchard. 1994. *Kids Come in All Languages: Reading Instruction for ESL Students*. Newark, DE: International Reading Association.

Staton, J. 1980. "Writing and Counseling: Using a Dialogue Journal." *Language Arts* 57 (5): 514–18.

———. 1985. "Using Dialogue Journals for Developing Thinking, Reading and Writing with Hearing-Impaired Students." *Volta Review* 87 (5): 127–54.

———. 1987. "The Power of Responding in Dialogue Journals." In T. Fulwiler, ed., *The Journal Book*, 47–63. Portsmouth, NH: Boynton/Cook Heinemann.

Stead, T. 2002. *Is That a Fact?: Teaching Nonfiction Writing, K–3*. Portland, ME: Stenhouse.

STEWARD, E. P. 1995. *Beginning Writers in the Zone of Proximal Development.* Hillsdale, NJ: Erlbaum.

TAYLOR, D. M. 1990. "Writing and Reading Literature in a Second Language." In N. Atwell ed., *Workshop 2: Beyond the Basal,* Portsmouth, NH: Heinemann.

THARP, R., and R. GALLIMORE. 1988. *Rousing Minds to Life: Teaching, Learning, and Schooling in Social Context.* New York: Cambridge University Press.

VAN DER VEER, R., AND J. VALSINER. 1993. *Understanding Vygotsky: A Quest for Synthesis.* Cambridge, UK: Blackwell.

VYGOTSKY, L. 1978. *Mind in Society: The Development of Higher Psychological Processes.* Cambridge, MA: Harvard University Press.

———. 1986. *Thought and Language.* Cambridge, MA: MIT Press.

WELLS, G. 1986. *The Meaning Makers: Children Learning Language and Using Language to Learn.* Portsmouth, NH: Heinemann.

WERTSCH, J. V., ed. 1985. *Culture, Communication and Cognition: Vygotskian Perspectives.* Cambridge, MA: Harvard University Press.

WISEMAN, A. M. 2003. "Collaboration, Initiation and Rejection: The Social Construction of Stories in a Kindergarten Class: The Social Complexity of Learning is Revealed During Read-Aloud and Journal Writing Time in a Classroom Where Students Are Encouraged to Interact with Peers as They Learn." *The Reading Teacher,* 56 (8): 802–900.

WOLLMAN-BONILLA, J. E. 1989. "Reading Journals: Invitations to Participate in Literature." *The Reading Teacher* 43 (1): 112–20.

WOOD, D., J. S. BRUNER, AND G. ROSS. 1976. "The Role of Tutoring in Problem Solving." *Journal of Child Psychology and Psychiatry* 17: 89–100.

ZINSSER, W. 1976. *On Writing Well: An Informal Guide to Writing Non-fiction.* New York: Harper & Row.